Matthew Arnold

The Great Prophecy of Israel's Restoration

Isaiah, Chapters 40-66; arranged and edited for young learners. 1872

Matthew Arnold

The Great Prophecy of Israel's Restoration
Isaiah, Chapters 40-66; arranged and edited for young learners. 1872

ISBN/EAN: 9783744795487

Printed in Europe, USA, Canada, Australia, Japan

Cover: Foto ©Lupo / pixelio.de

More available books at **www.hansebooks.com**

THE GREAT PROPHECY

OF

ISRAEL'S RESTORATION

(Isaiah, Chapters 40—66.)

Cambridge:
PRINTED BY C. J. CLAY, M.A.
AT THE UNIVERSITY PRESS.

A BIBLE-READING FOR SCHOOLS.

THE GREAT PROPHECY

OF

ISRAEL'S RESTORATION

(Isaiah, Chapters 40—66)

*ARRANGED AND EDITED FOR
YOUNG LEARNERS*

BY

MATTHEW ARNOLD, D.C.L.,

FORMERLY PROFESSOR OF POETRY IN THE UNIVERSITY OF OXFORD;
AND FELLOW OF ORIEL COLLEGE.

London:
MACMILLAN AND CO.
1872

[*All Rights reserved.*]

"Israel shall be saved in the Lord with an everlasting salvation."

PREFACE.

AT the very outset, the humbleness of what is professed in this little book cannot be set forth too strongly. With the aim of enabling English school-children to read as a connected whole the last twenty-seven chapters of Isaiah, without being frequently stopped by passages of which the meaning is almost or quite unintelligible, I have sought to choose, among the better meanings which have been offered for each of these passages, that which seemed the best, and to weave it into the authorised text in such a manner as not to produce any sense of strangeness or interruption. This is all that I have attempted; not to translate or to correct independently, for which my knowledge of Hebrew, —not more than sufficient to enable me in some degree to follow and weigh the reasons offered by others in support of their judgments,—and, indeed, my resources of all kinds, would be totally inadequate; but to use the work of more competent translators and correctors, to use it so as to remove difficulties in our authorised version which admit, many of them, of quite certain correction; and yet to leave the physiognomy and movement of the authorised version quite unchanged. Such a work of emendation may be, I hope, of a useful character, but it is certainly of a humble one; and the reader is especially begged to note that to this, and no more, does the present work aspire.

With like prominency must be set in view its provisional character. It makes no pretensions to be permanent. Persons of weight and of proved qualifications are now engaged in revising the Bible, and their revision must undoubtedly be looked to as that which, it is to be hoped, may obtain general currency. To have one version universally or almost universally received is of the greatest advantage. And their corrections will, probably, be much more extensive than those attempted here, and will extend far more to small points of detail; thus aiming at absolute correctness, at perfection. A version thus perfectly correct will most justly, if successful in other respects, supersede any private and partial attempts. Such a partial attempt is mine; an attempt, not to present an absolutely correct version of the series of chapters treated, but merely to remove such cause of disturbance as now, in the authorised version, prevents their being read connectedly, with understanding of what they mean, and with the profit and enjoyment that might else be drawn from them.

And why is the attempt made? It is made because of my conviction of the immense importance in education of what is called *letters;* of the side which engages our feelings and imagination. Science, the side which engages our faculty of exact knowledge, may have been too much neglected; more particularly this may have been so as regards our knowledge of nature. This is probably true of our secondary schools and universities. But on our *schools for the people* (by this good German name let us call them, to mark the overwhelmingly preponderant share which falls to them in the work of national education) the power of letters has hardly been brought to bear at all; certainly it has not been brought to bear in excess, as compared with the power of the natural sciences. And now, perhaps, it is less likely than ever to be brought to bear. The natural sciences are in high favour, it is felt that they have been unduly neglected, they have gifted and brilliant men for their advocates, schools for the people offer some special facilities for introducing them; on the other hand, the Bible, which would naturally be the great vehicle for conveying the power of letters into these schools, is withdrawn from the list of matters with which Government inspection concerns itself, and, so far, from attention. At the same time, good compendiums for the teaching of the natural sciences in schools for the people are coming forth; and the advantage to any branch of study of possessing good and compendious text-books it is impossible to overrate. The several natural sciences, too, from their limited and definite character, admit better of being advantageously presented by short text-books than such a wide and indefinite subject-matter,—nothing less than the whole history of the human spirit,—as that which belongs to letters; and this inherent advantage men of skill and talent, like the authors of the text-books I speak of, are just the people to turn to the best account. So that at the very time when the friends of the natural sciences have the public favour with them in saying to letters: "Give place, you have had more than your share of attention!" their case is still further improved by their being able to produce their own well-planned text-books for physics, and then to point to the literary textbooks now in use in schools for the people, and to say to the friends of letters: "And this is what you have to offer! this is what you make such a fuss over! this is what you keep our studies out in the cold for!" And in truth, while for those branches of study which belong partly to letters, partly to science,—language, geography, history,—our schools for the people have no text-books meriting comparison with the new text-books in physics, the schools are in worse plight still when we come to their means of acquainting their scholars with *letters* strictly so called, with poetry, philosophy, eloquence. A succession of pieces, not in general well-chosen, fragmentary, presented without any order or plan, and very ill comprehended by the pupil, is what our schools for the people give as *letters;* and the effect wrought by letters in these schools may be said, therefore, to be absolutely null.

It is through the apprehension, either of all literature,—the entire history of the human spirit,—or of a single great literature, or of a single great literary work, as a connected whole, that the real power of letters makes itself felt. Our leading secondary schools give the best share of their time to the literature of Greece and Rome. We shall not blame them for it; this literature is, indeed, only a part of the history of the human spirit, but it is a very important part. Yet how little, let us remark, do they conceive this literature as a whole! how little, therefore, do they get at its significance! how little do they *know* it! how little does it become a power, in their hands, towards wide and complete knowledge! But though in our secondary schools the scholar is not led to apprehend Greek and Latin literature as a whole, he is (and this is a very important matter) led and often enabled to lay hold of single great works, or connected portions of great works, of that literature, as wholes. Even supposing that the *Iliad* and *Odyssey* and *Æneid* and *Oresteia* are seldom entirely read at school, yet we must admit that portions of the *Iliad*, *Odyssey* and *Æneid*, and single plays of the *Oresteia*, do form important wholes by themselves, and that all the upper scholars in our chief schools have read them. What these scholars read or learn of English literature may be no more than what the scholars in our schools for the people read or learn of it,—short single pieces, or else bits detached here and there from longer works. But the last book of the *Iliad*, or the sixth book of the *Æneid*, or the *Agamemnon*, are considerable wholes in themselves, and these and other wholes of like beauty and magnitude they do read. And all their training has been such as to help them to understand what they read; they have always been hearing and learning (far too much so, many people think) about the objects and personages they meet with in it; Helicon and Parnassus are far more familiar names to them than Snowdon or Skiddaw; Troy and Mycenæ than Berlin or Vienna; Zeus and Phœbus than the gods of their own ancestors, Odin and Thor. So they are brought into "the presence and the power of greatness," as Wordsworth calls it, in these indisputably great works and great wholes; and when they are so brought, they may, if they attend, "perceive" it; they have the equipment of notions and of previous information qualifying them to perceive it. Now to know what Greece is, as a factor in the history of the human spirit, is one thing; to take in and enjoy the *Agamemnon* is another. But each is *a whole;* the two wholes are of a very different degree of value, nevertheless the second is a whole, and a worthy whole, as well as the first; and the apprehension of it leads, however rudimentarily, towards the first, and towards the whole of which the first is itself but a part. For it tends,—how much we cannot exactly determine, not much in one case, in another more than we could have believed possible,—it does tend, as Wordsworth again says, in lines which if not exactly good verse are at any rate good philosophy, to

> " Nourish imagination in her growth,
> And give the mind that apprehensive power,
> Whereby she is made quick to recognise
> The moral properties and scope of things."

In general, the scholars in our schools for the people come in contact with English literature in a mere fragmentary way, by short pieces or by odds and ends; and the power of a great work as a whole they have, therefore, no chance of feeling. But attempts are now sometimes made to acquaint them with some whole work, which is supposed to be clear and simple, such as, for instance, Goldsmith's *Deserted Village* or his *Traveller*. The *Deserted Village* and the *Traveller*, works of a very different rank from the same author's *Vicar of Wakefield*, may be called good poems, but they are good poems amongst poetry of the second or even the third order, and it would be absurd to speak of feeling the power of poetry through them as one feels it through the *Agamemnon*. But besides this, the modern literatures have so grown up under the influence of the literature of Greece and Rome, that the forms, fashions, notions, wordings, allusions of that literature have got deeply into them, and are an indispensable preparation for understanding them; now this preparation the scholars in our secondary schools, we have seen, have; all their training is such as to give it them, and it has thus passed into all the life and speech of what are called the cultivated classes. The people are without it; and how much of English literature is, therefore, almost unintelligible to the people, or at least to the people in their commencements of learning,—to the children of the people,—we can hardly perhaps enough convince ourselves. What the people can understand is such speech as:

"He sees his little lot the lot of all;"

but how small a proportion do lines like these bear, in Goldsmith's poetry, to lines like:

"The pregnant quarry teem'd with human form;"

or:

"See opulence, her grandeur to maintain,
Lead stern depopulation in her train;"

and everything of this kind falls on the ear of the people simply as words without meaning. Such diction is a reminiscence, bad or good, of Latin literature with its highly artificial manner; and such has been the influence of classical antiquity that this sort of diction, and the sort of notions that go with it, pervade in some shape or other nearly all our literature,—pervade works of infinitely higher merit than these poems of Goldsmith. And wherever this sort of diction and of notions presents itself, the people, one may say generally, are thrown out. A preparation is required which they have not had.

Only one literature there is, one great literature, for which the people have had a preparation,—the literature of the Bible. However far they may be from having a complete preparation for it, they have some; and it is the only great literature for which they have any. Their bringing up, what they have heard and talked of ever since they were born, have given them no sort of conversance with the forms, fashions, notions, wordings, allusions, of literature having its source in Greece and Rome; but they have given them a good deal of conversance with the forms, fashions, notions, wordings, allusions, of the Bible. Zion and Babylon are their Athens and Rome, their Ida and Olympus are Tabor and Hermon, Sharon is their Tempe; these and the like Bible names can reach their imagination, kindle trains of thought and remembrance in them. The elements with which the literature of Greece and Rome conjures, have no power on them; the elements with which the literature of the Bible conjures, have. Therefore I have so often insisted, in reports to the Education Department, on the need, if from this point of view only, for the Bible in schools for the people. If poetry, philosophy, and eloquence, if what we call in one word *letters*, are a power, and a beneficent wonder-working power, in education, through the Bible only have the people much chance of getting at poetry, philosophy, and eloquence. Perhaps I may here quote what I have at former times said : "Chords of power are touched by this instruction which no other part of the instruction in a popular school reaches, and chords various, not the single religious chord only. The Bible is for the child in an elementary school almost his only contact with poetry and philosophy. What a course of eloquence and poetry (to call it by that name alone) is the Bible in a school which has and can have but little eloquence and poetry! and how much do our elementary schools lose by not having any such course as part of their school-programme. All who value the Bible may rest assured that thus to know and possess the

Bible is the most certain way to extend the power and efficacy of the Bible."

I abstain from touching here on the political and ecclesiastical causes which obstruct such a use of the Bible in our popular schools. A cause more real is to be found in the conditions which at present rule our Bible-reading itself. If letters are a power, and if the first stage in feeling this power is, as we have seen, to apprehend certain great works as connected wholes, then it must be said that there are hardly any means at present for enabling young learners to get at this power through the Bible. And for two reasons. The Catholics taunted the Reformers with their *Bible-Babel;* and indeed that grand and vast miscellany which presents itself to us between the two covers of the Bible has in it something overpowering and bewildering. And its mass has never been grappled with, and separated, and had clear and connected wholes taken from it and arranged so that learners can use them, as the literature of Greece and Rome has. The Bible stands before the learner as an immense whole; yet to know the Bible as a whole, to know it in its historical aspect and in its connexion, to have a systematic acquaintance with its documents, is as great an affair as to know Greek literature as a whole; and we have seen how far our best education is from accomplishing this. But our best education does at any rate prepare the way for it, by presenting to the learner great connected wholes from Greek literature, like the *Agamemnon,* and does give the learner every help for understanding them; nothing or next to nothing of this kind has been done for the Bible. This is one reason why the fruitful use of the Bible, as literature, in our schools for the people, is at present almost impossible. The other reason lies in the defects of our translation, noble as it is; defects which abound most in those very parts of the Bible which, considered merely as literature, might have most power. Grant that we had definite wholes taken out of those parts of the Bible which exhibit its poetry and eloquence most conspicuously; grant that these wholes were furnished with all the explanations and helps for the young learner with which a Greek masterpiece is furnished; he would still again and again be thrown out by finding what he reads, though English, though his mother tongue, though always rhythmical, always nobly sounding, yet fail to be intelligible, fail to give a connexion with what precedes and follows, fail, as we commonly say, to *make sense*. This is a more serious matter than we might perhaps think. To be thrown out by a passage clean unintelligible, impairs and obscures the reader's understanding of much more than that particular passage itself; the entire connexion of ideas is broken for him and he has to begin again; and after several such passages have occurred in succession, he often reads languidly and hopelessly where he had begun to read with animation and joy; or, at any rate, even if the beauty of single phrases and verses still touches him, yet all grasp on his object as a whole is gone. But we have seen that it is by being apprehended *as a whole*, that the true power of a work of literature makes itself felt.

An ounce of practice, they say, is better than a pound of theory; and certainly one may talk for ever about the wonder-working power of letters, and yet produce no good at all, unless one really puts people in the way of feeling this power. The friends of physics do not content themselves with extolling physics; they put forth school-books by which the study of physics may be with proper advantage brought near to those who before were strangers to it; and they do wisely. For any one who believes in the civilising power of letters and often talks of this belief, to think that he has for more than twenty years got his living by inspecting schools for the people, has gone in and out among them, has seen that the power of letters never reaches them at all and that the whole study of letters is thereby discredited and its power called in question, and yet has attempted nothing to remedy this state of things, cannot but be vexing and disquieting. He may truly say, like the Israel of the prophet: "We have not wrought any deliverance in the earth!" and he may well desire to do something to pay his debt to popular education before he finally departs, and to serve it, if he can, in that point where its need is sorest, where he has always said its need was sorest, and where, nevertheless, it is as sore still as when he began saying this, twenty years ago. Even if what he does cannot be of service at once, owing to special prejudices and difficulties, yet these prejudices and difficulties years are almost sure to dissipate, and it may be of service hereafter.

The object, then, is to find some literary production of the highest order, which in our schools for the people can be studied and apprehended as a connected whole. It has been made out, I think, that we must go to the Bible for this; so the object will be to find in the Bible some whole, of admirable literary beauty in style and treatment, of manageable length, with defined limits; to present this to the learner in an intelligible shape, and to add such explanations and helps as may enable him to grasp it as a connected and complete work. Evidently the Old Testament offers more suitable matter for this purpose than the New. Its documents exhibit Hebrew literature in its perfection, while the New Testament does not pretend to exhibit the Greek language and literature in their perfection; the contents of the New Testament, moreover, almost entirely purport to be a plain record of events, or else to be epistles, and do not the least give themselves out as aspiring to the literary characters of poetry, rhythm, and eloquence; many parts of the Old Testament, on the other hand, do bear, and profess to bear, these characters. To the Old Testament, then, we had better go for what we want; and I think it is clear that nothing could more exactly suit our purpose than what the Old Testament gives us in the last twenty-seven chapters of the Book of Isaiah. The Hebrew language and genius, it is admitted by common consent, are seen in the Book of Isaiah at their perfection; this has naturally had its effect on the English translation, which nowhere perhaps rises to such beauty as in this Book. Then, whatever may be thought of the authorship of the last twenty-seven chapters, every one will allow that there comes a break between them and what goes immediately before them, and that they form a whole by themselves. And the whole which they form is large enough to exhibit a prolonged development and connexion, and yet is of manageable length, and comes within fixed limits. Add to which, it is a whole of surpassing interest; so that, while Isaiah is styled the greatest of the prophets, the evangelical prophet, and St. Jerome calls him not so much a prophet as an evangelist, and Ambrose told Augustine to read his prophecies the first thing after his conversion, and this prophet is of all Old Testament writers the one far most quoted in the New,—while all this is so, it is, moreover, in the last twenty-seven chapters that the greatest interest is reached; insomuch that out of thirty-four passages from him which Gesenius brings together as quoted in the New Testament, there are twenty-one from these last chapters against only thirteen from the rest of the Book. Finally, not only have the last twenty-seven chapters this poetical and this religious interest, but they have also an historical interest of the highest order; for they mark the very point where Jewish history, caught in the current of Cyrus's wars and policy, is carried into the great open stream of the world's history, never again to be separated from it.

But how to present these chapters to a young learner so that he may apprehend them? Evidently, as they stand in his Bible, they are baffling to him; and this is due partly to their arrangement, partly to obscurities in the translation. To shew how this is so, let us take a passage, not in this series of chapters, but yet evidently by its subject belonging to them,—let us take the 21st chapter of Isaiah down to the end of verse 10. Thus it stands in our Bibles :—

THE burden of the desert of the sea. As whirlwinds in the south pass through; *so* it cometh from the desert, from a terrible land.

2 A grievous vision is declared unto me; the treacherous dealer dealeth treacherously, and the spoiler spoileth. Go up, O Elam: besiege, O Media: all the sighing thereof have I made to cease.

3 Therefore are my loins filled with pain: pangs have taken hold upon me, as the pangs of a woman that travaileth: I was bowed down at the hearing *of it;* I was dismayed at the seeing *of it.*

4 My heart panted, fearfulness affrighted me: the night of my pleasure hath he turned into fear unto me.

5 Prepare the table, watch in the watch tower, eat, drink: arise, ye princes, *and* anoint the shield.

6 For thus hath the LORD said unto me, Go set a watchman, let him declare what he seeth.

7 And he saw a chariot with a couple of horsemen, a chariot of asses, and a chariot of camels; and he hearkened diligently with much heed:

8 And he cried, A lion: My lord, I stand continually upon

the watch-tower in the daytime, and I am set in my ward whole nights:

9 And behold, here cometh a chariot of men, with a couple of horsemen. And he answered and said, Babylon is fallen, is fallen; and all the graven images of her gods he hath broken unto the ground.

10 O my threshing, and the corn of my floor: that which I have heard of the LORD of hosts, the God of Israel, have I declared unto you.

And then the chapter goes on without any interruption, in verses of just the same look, to a wholly different matter.

Now the learner in our schools for the people, who has the bare text of a common Bible and nothing more, may perceive that there is something grand in this passage, but he cannot possibly understand it; and this is due partly to the want of explanations, partly to the arrangement, partly to obscurity in the translation. He requires to be told first, as a learner would be told before reading an ode of Pindar, what it is all about; he requires to have the passage separated for him from that with which it has no connexion; and he requires to have the text made much clearer, both in its words and in its punctuation.

To supply explanations, it may be thought, is a matter which need not embarrass us much; but the same cannot be said of re-arranging and correcting. It must be remembered that in dealing with the English Bible, we are dealing with a work consecrated in the highest degree by long use and deep veneration; and we are dealing with it not for the benefit of the learned, but for the benefit of our schools for the people, where we have not much readiness for change to expect, but rather much resistance to innovation. As to arrangement, therefore, we must not cut and carve too freely; a book, for instance, like *The Psalms Chronologically Arranged, by Four Friends,*—with its Psalter turned, so to speak, inside out, with its re-distribution, its novel lettering, its interpolation of headings in archaic English by the Four Friends,—one can hardly imagine a book like this, useful as it really is, coming at present into general use in schools; the changes it makes are too glaring and radical. We have not even ventured to detach from their place, and to print with the last twenty-seven chapters, those earlier chapters of the Book of

Isaiah, the 13th with the 14th down to the end of the 23rd verse, the 21st down to the end of the 10th verse, the chapters from the beginning of the 24th to the end of the 27th, and the 34th and 35th chapters; though these chapters are certainly connected by their subject with the concluding series, are boldly printed with them by recent translators, and should at any rate be read in connexion with them by every student who wishes to apprehend the concluding series fully. But this concluding series forms a connected whole by itself, even as it now stands in our Bibles; by itself it does give us, in strictness, what we want; and to take other separated chapters out of their place, and print them in a new order, might fairly enough be called tearing the Book of Isaiah to pieces and recomposing it by private authority; and a book for elementary schools ought not to lay itself open to a reproach of this kind. The same is to be said of the novel way of dividing, organising, and presenting their single Psalms or single chapters, which recent translators, following Professor Ewald, have adopted: in him and them, and for his and their purpose, we may acquiesce in it; but for our purpose it changes the face of the Bible too startlingly and entirely. The divisions in our common Bibles, however, do mark too little the connexion of the sense, do often break it too arbitrarily, and of themselves create difficulties for the reader. This will not be denied; but the question is, how to apply a remedy without innovating overmuch. Now it so happened that I had for many years been in the habit of using a Bible* where the numbers of the chapters are marked at the side and do not interpose a break between chapter and chapter; and where the divisions of the verses, being numbered in like manner at the side of the page, not in the body of the verse, and being numbered in very small type, do not thrust themselves forcibly on the attention. Breaks between the chapters, too, this Bible admits, but only when the sense seems urgently to call for them; and sometimes, on the same motive, it even breaks a verse in the middle. And it had always struck me how much more connected and comprehensible the sense of the Bible, and particularly of certain

---

* Perhaps I may be allowed here to mention, what to me at least will always be very interesting, that this Bible was given to me by the late Mr Keble, my godfather

parts of the Bible such as the Prophetical Books and the Epistles, appeared in this arrangement than in that of our common Bibles; insomuch that here things would often look comparatively lucid and hanging together, which in our common Bibles looked fragmentary and obscure. Well, then, it suggested itself to me to try, for conveying to unskilled learners the series of chapters I had chosen, this mode of arrangement, extending it a little and simplifying it a little; extending it by using breaks, if this seemed required by the sense, a little more frequently; and simplifying it by getting rid of italics, signs, references, and all apparatus of this sort, which readers such as we have in view hardly ever understand, and are more distracted than helped by. So we might hope to exhibit this series of chapters in a way to give a clue to their connexion and sense, yet without making them look too odd and novel.

So far for the arrangement: but even a more important matter was correction, since an unintelligible passage, baffling the reader and throwing him out, will often, as we have said, spoil a whole chapter for him, and there are many such passages in the authorised version. To avoid this check in reading the grand series of chapters at the end of Isaiah, I had gradually made for my own use the corrections which seemed indispensable; these corrections, after having been carefully revised, are adopted in the text now offered. And by indispensable corrections I mean this: corrections which enable us to read the authorised version without being baffled and thrown out. The urgent matter, of course, is to get rid of the stoppage and embarrassment created by such things as: "He made his grave with the wicked...*because* he had done no violence;" or as: "That prepare a table for *that troop*, and that furnish the drink-offering for *that number*."* A clear sense is the indispensable thing; even where the authorised version seems wrong, if its words give a clear sense, I have almost always left them unaltered. Sometimes, however, when the right correction seems to give a sense either markedly clearer or markedly higher in poetic propriety and beauty than the authorised version, I have corrected; but only if both the correction seemed certain, and the gain in clearness, or in beauty, or in both, undeniable.

* Isaiah liii. 9, and lxv. 11.

For example. I think it certain that at verse 15 of the 65th chapter the right rendering is: "And ye shall leave your name for a curse unto my chosen, *So may the Lord God slay thee!*"—the words in italics being the words of the curse, as in Jeremiah xxix: "Of them (Zedekiah and Ahab) shall be taken up a curse by all the captivity of Judah which are in Babylon, saying, *The Lord make thee like Zedekiah and Ahab!*" But the authorised version gives a perfectly clear sense: "And ye shall leave your name for a curse unto my chosen; for the LORD God shall slay thee;"—and I have therefore left this as it stands. Again, at v. 18 of the 66th chapter, I think the right rendering almost certainly is: "But I —— their works and their thoughts!—it shall come, that I will gather all nations," &c.; the expression being, as Professor Ewald explains it, a broken, indignant one, with this sense:—Utterly to confound and shame the expectations and practices of the faithless, idol-seeking Jews (who have been the subject of the preceding verse), idolatrous nations themselves shall come and worship me. But the authorised version: "For I know their works and their thoughts" (referring to the idolatrous Jews of the preceding verse);—and then, after a pause, passing to another subject: "It shall come, that I will gather all nations,"—gives, perhaps, a yet clearer sense, though, I believe, not the right sense; but the sense given being good and clear, I without hesitation feel bound to abstain from change. It may seem at variance with this that, for instance, in the last clause of the 46th chapter: "I will place salvation in Zion for Israel my glory," which is quite clear, I have yet allowed myself to make a change, and to substitute: "I will give salvation to Zion; to Israel my glory." But this is because, while the change appears, from the law of parallelism in Hebrew poetry, perfectly certain, the observance here of this law gives, at the same time, a decided gain in poetic propriety and beauty. So in verse 14 of the 43rd chapter: "I have sent to Babylon and have brought down all their nobles, and the Chaldeans, whose cry is in the ships." This cannot be right, but it gives a sense which may be made out; we may refer to what Heeren says of the maritime trade of Babylon in the Persian Gulf, and explain the last clause of the Chaldean fleets there, and of the joyful hailing and shouting of the sailors. But we so little associate Babylon with a maritime trade and fleets, that this sense for the passage is a strained and unacceptable one; whereas the more correct rendering: "I have sent to Babylon, and do make them all to flee away, and the Chaldeans upon the ships of their pleasure," associates Babylon with her great feature,—the river and the use of the river; and so gives a sense, if not absolutely plainer, yet poetically much more natural and more pleasing. Here therefore is a case where our rules justify a change.

But when a change, however pleasing and ingenious, depends on taking license to alter by guess the original text, I have regarded it as quite forbidden. There is a difficult expression in verse 17 of the 66th chapter, "behind one tree in the midst," where the word *tree* is supplied by our English translators, and the original has only "behind one in the midst;" now, the Hebrew word for *behind* nearly resembles the Hebrew word for *one*, and Professor Ewald proposes to read, in place of the word for *one*, the word for *behind* repeated; so that the meaning will be: "Back, back in the innermost sanctuary!"—a cry of recoil of the idol-serving and superstitious renegade Jews at the approach of their uninitiated, and, as they thought, profane countrymen. This suits well with the "I am holier than thou!" attributed to the same renegades, and as a conjectural emendation it is highly plausible and attractive; still, a conjectural emendation it is, and therefore, as I consider, not permissible for our purpose here. All we may do is to supply a word giving a better sense than the word *tree*, and such a word is *chief*,—the ringleader or chief in the processions and ceremonies held in the sacred gardens.

So it will be evident that our range for alteration is strictly limited; indeed, it may almost be said, in general, to be restricted to those cases where in the authorised version there is unintelligibility or ambiguity baffling the reader and throwing him out. A translator whose aim is purely scientific, to render his original with perfect accuracy, will have much more latitude, and no one can blame him for taking it; but then the public he must propose to himself is different. Possibly too, as has been already said, a body of Bible-revisers acting by public authority ought to take much more latitude, and to correct the old version not only where it is unintelligible, but also wherever they think it in error. Perhaps they ought; but it is clear that no private translator, taking such latitude, could have any hope of getting his work admitted into schools for the people. And the reader in these schools we want to benefit, not the learned. And our object is such that to retain as far as possible the old text of the Bible is very desirable, nay, almost indispensable; we want to enable him to apprehend, as a whole, a literary work of the highest order. And the Book of Isaiah, as it stands in our Bibles, is this in a double way; by virtue of the original it is a monument of the Hebrew genius at its best, and by virtue of the translation it is a monument of the English language at its best. Some change must be made for clearness' sake, without which the work cannot be apprehended as a whole; but the power of the English version must not be sacrificed, must, if possible, be preserved intact; and though every corrector says this, and pays his compliment to the English version, yet few proceed to act upon the rule, or seem to know how hard it is to act upon it when we alter at all, and why it is hard. Let us try and make clear to ourselves exactly what the difficulty is.

The English version has created certain sentiments in the reader's mind, and these sentiments must not be disturbed, if the new version is to have the power of the old. Surely this consideration should rule the corrector in determining whether or not he should put *Jehovah* where the old version puts *Lord*. Mr. Cheyne, the recent translator of Isaiah,—one of that new band of Oxford scholars who so well deserve to attract our interest, because they have the idea, which Oxford has had so far too little, of separated and systematised studies,—Mr. Cheyne writes for teachers, and his object is scientific, to render the original with exactness. This is well, and it is a line a translator may very properly and usefully take; only then he should not talk of governing himself, in making changes, by "the affectionate reverence with which the Authorised Version is so justly regarded," for his changes are such as to get rid of the effect and sentiment of this version entirely. But how the Four Friends, who evidently, by their style of comment, mean their book for religious use, for habitual readers of the Psalms, and who even take, because of this design, the Prayer-Book version as their basis; how they can have permitted themselves to substitute *Jehovah* for *Lord* passes one's comprehension. Probably because they were following Professor Ewald; but his object is scientific. To obtain general acceptance by English Christians, who that considers what the name in question represents to these, what the Psalms are to them, what a place the expression, *The Lord*, fills in the Psalms and in the English Bible generally, what feelings and memories are entwined with it, and what the force of sentiment is,—who that considers all this, would allow himself, in a version of the Psalms meant for popular use, to abandon the established expression, *The Lord?* And *Jehovah* is in any case a bad substitute for it, because to the English reader it does not carry its own meaning with it, and has even, which is fatal, a mythological sound. *The Eternal*, which the French versions use, is far preferable. *The Eternal* is in itself, no doubt, a better rendering of Jehovah than *The Lord;* in disquisition and criticism, where it is important to keep as near as we can to the exact sense of words, *The Eternal* may be introduced with advantage; and whoever has heard Jewish school-children use it, as they do, in repeating the Commandments in English, cannot but have been struck and satisfied with the effect of the rendering. But for English school-children, and, indeed, for all English people using the Bible except with a special scientific purpose, *The Lord* is surely an expression consecrated; the meaning which it in itself carries is a meaning contained in the original name, even though it may be possible to render this original more adequately; but, besides the contents which a term carries in itself, we must consider the contents with which men, in long and reverential use, have filled it; and therefore we say that *The Lord* any literary corrector of the English Bible must retain, because of the sentiments this expression has created in the English reader's mind, and firmly fixed there.

It is in deference to these pre-established sentiments in the reader that we prefer, so long as the sense is well preserved, for any famous passage of our chapters which is cited in the New Testament, the New Testament rendering, because this rendering will be to the English reader the more familiar, and touches more chords. For instance, in the 2nd verse of the 43rd chapter, *He shall not cry nor lift up* is the Old Testament rendering; *He shall not clamour nor cry* might in itself be better, but *He shall not strive nor cry* seems to us best of all, because the New Testament has made it familiar. For the same reason, it is with extreme reluctance that we alter any signally familiar wording; the change in the first clause of the 53rd chapter is the only such change I can recall, and it will hardly be believed what a struggle it cost me to make it. Considerations of clearness, and of the sense and connexion of the whole, are in the last resort to govern us; now, to make the prophet say, as one of the sinful people, *Who believed what we heard?* instead of making him say, as a prophet of God, *Who hath believed our report?* suits much better in connexion with what immediately follows, where he manifestly speaks as one of the sinful people. Undoubtedly, in our series of chapters, he speaks in both capacities; but it seems too baffling that he should speak in the one capacity in the first verse of a chapter, and then in the other capacity in the five verses which instantly follow. Add to this, that the meaning we have adopted joins the verse in a very striking way to the intimately connected last verse of the preceding chapter. Still, we tried at first to keep the old wording, *Who believed our report?* explaining in a note that *our report* meant not the report *we gave* but the report *we had*. This, however, evidently takes all clearness out of the expression; so in deference, first, to the sense and connexion of the whole, and then to clearness, we finally were driven to the change made. All this is mentioned to shew what deference we really feel to be due to the pre-established sentiments above spoken of.

But perhaps there would not be much difficulty if we had only to avoid rash change in these marked cases. There is a far subtler difficulty to be contended with. The English Bible is a tissue, a fabric woven in a certain style, and a style which is admirable. When the version was made, this style was *in the air;* get a body of learned divines, and set them down to translate, the right meaning they might often have difficulty with, but the right style was pretty well sure to come of itself. This style is in the air no longer; that makes the real difficulty of the learned divines now at work in Westminster. And exactly in what the style consists, and what will impair it, and what sort of change can be brought into it, and to what amount, without destroying it, no learning can tell them; they must trust to a kind of tact. Every one agrees that in correcting the English Bible (we do not now speak of re-translation in an aim of scientific exactness) you must not change its style; the question is, what kinds of alteration *do* change its style? By two kinds of alteration, it may be affirmed, you change its style; you change it if you destroy *the character of the diction*, and you change it if you destroy *the balance of the rhythm*. Either is enough; and one has only to state these two conditions to make it clear how entirely the observance of them must be a matter of tact, and cannot be ensured by any external rules. It is often said that no word ought to be used in correcting the English Bible which is not there already. This is pedantry; no word must be used which does not *suit* the Bible diction, but plenty of words may suit it which do not happen to be there already. And after all, what have you gained, if you get a word which is ever so much a Bible word, and put it in so as to spoil the rhythm? the style of the Bible is equally changed, whether it is the character of its diction that you destroy, or the balance of its rhythm.

Thus quite petty changes may have a great and fatal effect; the mass of a passage may be left (and this is what a corrector generally understands by shewing "affectionate reverence for the Authorised Version"), and yet by altering a word or two the Bible style may be more changed than if the passage had been half re-written. I name Bishop Lowth with the highest respect; he, Vitringa, and the Jewish commentator Aben-Ezra, are perhaps the three men who, before the labours of the Germans in our century, did most to help the study of Isaiah. And what Lowth did was due mainly to fine tact and judgment in things of poetry and literature; this enabled him to make his just and fruitful remarks on the structure of the composition of the Hebrew prophets, and on the literary character of the whole Hebrew Scriptures. And he could point out, in Sebastian Castellio's Latin version, the fault of "the loss of Hebrew simplicity, the affectation of Latin elegance," and observe that ' to this even the barbarism of the Vulgate is preferable." And he saw the merit, both in diction and in rhythm, of our authorised English version: "As to the style and language," he says, "it admits but of little improvement;" all he proposed to himself was to "correct and perfect it." But in good truth *style*, such as the beginning of the 17th century knew it, was at the end of the 18th century no longer in the air; else how could a man of Lowth's sound critical principles and fine natural tact have thought that he perfected " Speak ye *comfortably* to Jerusalem " by making it " Speak ye *animating words* to Jerusalem ;" or " *Taught him knowledge*" by substituting "*Impart to him science;*" or "Hear now this, *thou that art given to pleasures, that dwellest carelessly*," by " Hear now this, *O thou voluptuous, that sittest in security;*" or " Yet did we *esteem him stricken*," by " Yet we *thought him judicially stricken;*" or " When thou shalt make his soul *an offering for sin*," by " If his soul shall make *a propitiatory sacrifice;*" or " My salvation is *near to come*," by "My salvation is *near, just ready to come*"? Surely this is not perfecting but marring.

So, too, Mr. Cheyne may be rendering his original with more accuracy when he writes: " He shall bring forth *religion truthfully*," instead of " He shall bring forth *judgment unto truth;*" but he must not imagine that he is here making a trifling change in the wording of the old version, for he destroys its character altogether. When he writes: " He shall not fail nor be discouraged till he have set religion in the earth, and the sea-coasts wait for his doctrine," he must not imagine that he is making a slight change in the rhythm of " He shall not fail nor be discouraged, till he have set judgment in the earth: and the isles shall wait for his law," for he destroys the balance of the rhythm altogether. He may or may not be expressing the prophet's meaning in appropriate English, which he says is his design, when he puts " Who hath believed our *revelation*," for " Who hath believed our report," or " He was *tormented, but he suffered freely, and* opened not his mouth," for " He was *oppressed, and he was afflicted, yet he* opened not his mouth;" but he is not governing himself by "the affectionate reverence with which the Authorised Version is so justly regarded," for he is changing its effect totally. And this, though there may be only a word or two altered, or though the new and imported words may be honest Bible words like the old.

Hence we see how delicate is the matter we are touching,

when we take in hand the authorised version to correct it; and as there is so much risk, it seems the safest way, first indeed to be very shy of correcting needlessly; but then, if there is need to correct, to keep if possible the cast of phraseology and the fall of sentence already given by the old version, and to correct within the limits of these, transgressing the limits of neither. For instance: " He was taken from prison and from judgment, and who shall declare his generation? for he was cut off out of the land of the living; for the transgression of my people was he stricken." This needs correction, for it gives no clear sense; but it possesses a cast of phraseology and a fall of sentence which are marked, which we all know well and should be loath to lose. Mr. Cheyne substitutes: "From oppression and from judgment was he taken,—and as for his generation, who considered that he was cut off out of the land of the living, for the transgression of my people he was stricken." This is hardly clearer, indeed, than the old version; still, the old version's cast of phraseology is on the whole maintained, but what has become of its fall of sentence? Surely it is better to try and keep this too; and if we say: "He was taken from prison and from judgment; and who of his generation regarded it, why he was cut off out of the land of the living? for the transgression of my people was he stricken!"—we at least try to keep it. It would be easy to translate the verse more literally by changing its words and rhythm more radically; but what we should thus gain in one way is less than what we should lose in another.

However, the safest way, of course, is to abstain from change; and the trial of the corrector is in deciding where to make change and where not. For the public and authorised corrector the latitude is greater, as I have said, than for an attempt like ours. *I will destroy and devour at once*, in verse 14 of chapter 42, is perfectly clear and gives a tolerable sense, so we have kept it; but it is certainly not at all the sense of the original, and public and authorised correctors would be right in changing it. But I doubt whether any corrector should, merely for the sake of being more exactly literal, change good words which give the general sense of the original; for example, in the second verse of the first chapter of our series, "*Her iniquity is pardoned*" sufficiently conveys the general sense; "*Her sin-offering is accepted*" is more exact, but there is no adequate reason to change. But the next clause, "*She hath received at the Lord's hand double for all her sins,*" is ambiguous; it may mean, her punishments are twice as much as her sins, or it may mean, her blessings are twice as much as her punishments; it does mean the latter, but the words would lend themselves to the former meaning more readily. Mr. Cheyne makes no change at all; he ought to have made a change. Lowth substitutes, "*She shall receive at the hand of Jehovah blessings double to the punishment of all her sins;*" the right sense is given, but the rhythm of the old version is gone. Whereas the changing only one word would have left the rhythm as it was, and yet have made the meaning quite clear: "*She shall receive at the Lord's hand double for all her* rue."

Lowth in this passage changes the tense of the verb, and here too is a point where, it should be noticed, great heed is requisite. Very often, in the Hebrew prophets and poets, the time is a kind of indeterminate one, neither strictly present, past, nor future; they speak of God's action, and the time of God's action is the time of a general law, which we can without impropriety make present, past, or future, as we will. So in Horace's famous lines declaring how regularly punishment overtakes the wicked: "*Raro antecedentem scelestum deseruit pede pœna claudo;*" the verb here might almost equally well, as far as the sense is concerned, be *deseruit,* or *deseret,* or *deserit,*—hath abandoned, shall abandon, or doth abandon. Very often, where the time is of this kind, the form of the Hebrew verb does not make it certain for us, as in Latin, how we shall render; the authorised version, having in view the nature, as popularly conceived, of prophetical speech, always leans to the future. Some modern translators uniformly lean the other way; but in all cases where the sense is not certainly brought out better by one tense than another, the corrector of the English Bible had better, in my opinion, hold his hand; for to change the tense is, very often, to change the rhythm. In the particular text of our prophet which we have just been discussing, the authorised version has the verb in the past tense: " She *hath received* at the Lord's hand double for all her sins." Lowth changes it to the future: " She *shall receive;*" but the present is more vivid: " She *receiveth,*" for this represents the compensation as actually taking place and begun. But it is the future tense in the authorised version which nine times out of ten raises the question of change; for example: "The isles *shall wait* for his law," where we have rendered, "Far lands *wait* for his law." For, surely, waiting is already prospective enough without weakening it by making it more prospective still; so that here, it seems to me, the meaning gains decidedly if we change the tense to the present. But except where there is a decided gain of this sort, I have let the futures of the old version stand.

So, too, as to that often recurring expression, *the isles, the islands*. This rendering is consecrated by its long and universal use; not only our Bibles have it, but the Septuagint and the Vulgate have it also, and Luther has it. And it is noble and poetical; *coasts, strands*, is more literal, and is the rendering preferred by the modern German translators, and by Mr. Cheyne following them. But where the coasts and isles of the Mediterranean are alone intended, and no stress is meant to be specially laid on their remoteness, *isles*, which is more distinct and beautiful than *coasts*, seems preferable; but sometimes remoteness is an important part of the idea, and then neither *isles* nor *coasts* quite satisfies. This is so in the passage quoted a little way back: "*The isles* shall wait for his law." The full meaning is not here brought out; nor does Mr. Cheyne bring it out any more by "*The sea-coasts* wait for his doctrine." Lowth has: "*The distant nations* shall earnestly wait for his law;" and this is undoubtedly the meaning, only *distant nations* is prosaic, and breaks the character of the Bible style. Therefore, where remoteness seems a prominent part of the idea, we have used the rendering *far lands;* as here: "*Far lands* wait for his law." But in general we have retained the well-known *isles*.

And the same with those noble and consecrated expressions, *judgment, righteousness;* we have hardly ever meddled with them. To talk, like Mr. Cheyne, of setting *religion* in the earth, instead of setting *judgment* in the earth, seems to us wanton; but in our series of chapters there are several places where *saving health, salvation*, undoubtedly renders the original more truly than the *righteousness* of the English Bible. Here we have hesitated, and there was considerable inducement to change; still, the notions of *righteousness* and of *the salvation belonging to righteousness* do in our prophet so run into one another, and the word righteousness in the English Bible is so noble a word in itself, and so weighty an element of rhythm, that again and again, even after changing, we have gone back to it.

In short, we have had a most lively sense of the risk one runs in touching a great national monument like the English Bible; and how one is apt, by changes which seem little, to mar and destroy utterly. If we are asked why we could not wait for the revision promised by Convocation, we answer that two or three more school-generations will have gone before this revision comes, and even then it will not give us what for our special purpose we want,—one self-contained portion of the Bible, detached to stand as a great literary whole. But we will add, too, that we think there is a danger with any body of modern correctors of changing too much, and of thinking that little things, especially, may be freely changed without harm; and we are conscious of an "affectionate reverence" for the diction and rhythm of the English Bible, greater even, perhaps, than that of many of the official revisers,—a reverence which, while for our purpose *some* change in the text is needed, makes us eager, notwithstanding, to preserve its total effect unimpaired, and binds us, in this aim, to a moderation in altering much more than commonly scrupulous. After all, the total number of changes made is considerable, for clearness required it; but nothing would be so gratifying as to find that a reader had gone from the beginning of the chapters to the end without noticing anything different from what he was accustomed to, except that he was not perplexed and thrown out as formerly. No corrector should wish to claim any property in the English Bible; that work, and the glory of it, belongs to the old translators, and theirs, even if their work is amended, it should remain. Even their punctuation one would gladly retain; but this one finds oneself more and more, the more one deals with it, obliged in the interest of clearness and effect to alter.

We must still add a word about the notes and explanations. This little book is meant for the young, and has no business to discuss, or even to raise, questions which are in dispute between different schools of Biblical interpreters. There ought to be nothing in it which should hinder the adherent of any school of Biblical interpretation or of religious belief from using it, and from putting it into the hands of children. The authorship of our series of chapters is a vexed question; and undoubtedly I believe that the author of the earlier part of the Book of Isaiah was not the author of these last chapters. There is nothing to forbid a member of the Church of England, or, for that matter, a member of the Church of Rome either, or a member of the Jewish Synagogue, from holding such a belief; but it is not a belief which a work like the present has to concern itself with. Our work ought simply to place itself, in presenting the last twenty-seven chapters of Isaiah, at the moment of history where the contents of them become simplest, most actual, most striking; now, this moment evidently is the moment of Cyrus's attack on Babylon and contemplated restoration of the Jews. This is the moment when to the Jewish nation itself these chapters must undoubtedly have come out with far more clearness and fulness than could have been possible a hundred and fifty years earlier, when the matters handled were mere predictions of unknown future events. The greatness of Hebrew prophecy, or even its special character, are not concerned here. In my belief the unique grandeur of the Hebrew prophets consists, indeed, not in the curious foretelling of details, but in the unerring vision with which they saw, the unflinching boldness and sublime force with which they said, that the great unrighteous kingdoms of the heathen could not stand, and that the world's salvation lay in a recourse to the God of Israel. But, anyhow, the general prophecy that the great unrighteous kingdoms of the heathen could not stand was all that could in the time of Ahaz be fully effective; the full effect of all the particulars in our twenty-seven chapters must have been reserved for the time when these particulars began visibly to explain themselves by being produced and fulfilled. This every one must admit; even those who believe that the prophecy existed in the reign of Ahaz, a century and a half before the conquests of Cyrus, will allow that at the moment of the conquests of Cyrus its significance would be brought out much more fully. And therefore we desire to place the reader in the position of a Jew reading the chapters at that critical moment, when the wars and revolutions with which they deal had a nearness, grandeur, and reality they could not have before or afterwards. But any one is free to suppose, if he likes, that these chapters, so apposite and actual at that moment, were an old prediction which had been in the possession of the Jews long before; whether this was so or not, whether it is consistent with the true nature of Hebrew prophecy that this should have been so, are questions into which the present work does not enter, and ought not to enter.

Some persons will say, probably, that the notes and explanations confine themselves too much to the local and temporary side of these prophecies; that the prophecies have two sides, a side towards their nation and its history at the moment, and a side towards the future and all mankind; and that this second side is by much the more important. I admit unreservedly that these prophecies have a scope far, far beyond their primary historical scope, that they have a secondary, eternal scope, and that this scope is far, far the more important. To deny this would, in my judgment, shew a very bad critic; but we must make a distinction. There is a substratum of history and literature in the Bible which belongs to science and schools; there is an application of the Bible and an edification by the Bible which belongs to religion and churches. Some people say the Bible altogether belongs to the Church, not the school. This is an error; the Bible's application and edification belong to the Church, its literary and historical substance to the school. Other people say, that the Bible does indeed belong to school as well as Church, but that its application and edification are inseparable from its literature and history. This is an error, they *are* separable. And though its application and edification are what matter to a man far most (we say so in all sincerity), are what he mainly lives by, yet it so happens that it is just in this application and edification that religious differences arise. For things do really lend themselves to far greater diversity in the way of application of them, and edification by them, than in the way of their primary historical and literary interpretation. To take an example which will come home to all Protestants: Dr. Newman, in one of those charming Essays which he has of late rescued for us, quotes from the 54th chapter of Isaiah the passage beginning, *I will lay thy stones with fair colours and thy foundations with sapphires,* as a prophecy and authorisation of the sumptuosities of the Church of Rome. This is evidently to use the passage in the way of application. Protestants will say that it is a wrong use of it; but to Dr. Newman their similar use of passages about the beast, and the scarlet woman, and Antichrist, will seem equally wrong; and in these cases of application who shall decide? But as to the historical substratum, the primary sense of the passage Dr Newman quotes, what dissension can there be? who can deny that in the first instance, however we may apply them afterwards and whether this after-application be right or wrong, the prophet's words apply to the restored Zion? Then it is said, that those who lay stress on this primary application of the words of the Bible reject and disparage the secondary. So far from it, that the secondary application of the 53rd chapter of Isaiah to Christ both *is* incomparably more important than its now obscure primary historical application, and will be admitted by every sound critic to be so. But, finally, it is said that the historical and literary substratum in the Bible is, then, relatively unimportant. And this belief is wide-spread and genuine; but we answer,—and here is the justification of works like the present,—that absolutely, at any rate, it is of very high importance; that without this historical and literary substructure, the full religious significance of the Bible can never build itself up for our minds, and that those who most value the Bible's religious significance ought most to regard this substructure. Admirably true are these words of Goethe, so constant a reader of the Bible that his free-thinking friends reproached him for wasting his time over it: "I am convinced that the Bible becomes even more beautiful the more one understands it; that is, the more one gets insight to see, that every word, which we take generally and make special application of to our own wants, has had, in connexion with certain circumstances, with certain relations of time and place, a particular, directly individual reference of its own."

So that though our series of chapters, like the Bible in general, contains more, much more, than what our notes chiefly deal with, yet this too, nevertheless, is of very high importance and leads up to that *more;* and besides it belongs to school, and can be taught and learnt without offering ground for those religious disputes to which a more extended interpretation of the Bible often gives rise. What disputes it offers ground for are of the sort which may arise out of any historical and literary enquiry, and they are the fewer the more the enquiry is conducted in an unassuming and truly scientific manner; when that only is called certain which is really certain, and that which is conjecture, however plausible, is allowed to be but conjecture. It sets Bible-readers against all historical and literary investigation of the Bible, when novelties are violently and arrogantly imposed upon them without sufficient grounds. No one who has been studying the Book of Isaiah should close his studies without paying homage to the German critics who in this century have accomplished so much for that Book; and to two great names, perhaps, above all,—Gesenius and Ewald. Professor Ewald exhibits in a signal degree, over and above all his learning, two natural gifts,—the historical sense and the poetical sense; the poetical sense, in my opinion, in a yet higher degree than the historical. For the literary and historical investigation of the Bible he has done wonders; yet perhaps no one has done more to offend plain readers with such investigation, by a harsh and splenetic dogmatism, as unphilosophical as it is unpleasing. His great fault is that he will insist on our taking as certainty what is and must be but conjecture. He knows just when each chapter and portion of a chapter was written, just where another prophet comes in and where he leaves off; he knows it the more confidently the more another critic has known differently. But *know* in these cases he cannot, he can but guess plausibly; and sometimes his guess, which he gives as certain, has much to discredit even its plausibility. Our series of chapters, for instance, he insists we shall believe was written in Egypt, not Babylon, because Persia is called in it *the north*, and Persia is north to Egypt, not to Babylon. How strange that it never occurred to him, before thus making a certainty where there can be none, that Persia is north to *Zion;* and that for the Jewish exile in Babylon, Zion, the centre of his thoughts, may well also have been the centre of his geography!

The more we are content to let our text speak for itself, to try and follow its intentions and elucidate them without imposing on it ours, the better critics we shall be certainly, but also the less risk we shall run of indisposing ordinary readers to Biblical criticism by rash changes or by assertions pressed too far. There can hardly be a more interesting enquiry than who the *servant of God*, so often mentioned in our series of chapters, really was. We all know the secondary application to Christ, often so striking; but certainly this was not the primary application; who was originally meant? the purged idealised Israel? or a single prophet, the writer of the book? or the whole body of prophets? or the pious and persisting part of the Jewish nation? or the whole mass of the Jewish nation? It may safely be said that *all* these are meant, sometimes the one of them, sometimes the other; and the best critic is he who does not insist on being more precise than his text, who follows his text with docility, allows it to have its way in meaning sometimes one and sometimes the other, and is intelligent to discern when it means one and when the other. But a German critic elects one out of these several meanings, and will have the text decidedly mean that one and no other. He does not reflect that in his author's own being all these characters were certainly blended: the ideal Israel, his own personal individuality, the character of representative of his order, the character of representative of the pious and faithful part of the nation, the character (who that knows human nature can doubt it?) of representative of the sinful mass of the nation. How then, when the prophet came to speak, could *God's servant* fail to be all these by turns? No doubt, the most important and beautiful of these characters is the character of the ideal Israel, and Professor Ewald has shewn poetical feeling in seizing on it, and in eloquently developing its significance. Gesenius, Professor Ewald's inferior in genius, but how superior in good temper and freedom from jealousy and acrimony! seizes in like manner on the character of representative of the order of prophets. But both of them make the object of their selection a hobby, and ride it too hard; and when they come to the perilous opening of the 49th chapter, both of them permit themselves, in order to save their hobby, to tamper with the text. These are the proceedings which give rise to disputes, cause offence, make historical and literary criticism of the Bible to be regarded with suspicion; a faithful, simple, yet discriminative following of one's author and his text might avoid them all.

We have been too long; but our attempt is new, and needed

explanation. One or two words of yet more special explanation have yet to be added. References, except to the passages quoted from the Bible, are hardly ever given in our notes; they are written for readers who in general will have no book of reference but their Bible. A variety of interpretations of any passage is hardly ever given; one interpretation is adopted, and the rest are left without notice. This is not because I consider the interpretation to be in all cases certain, but because the notes are written for those who are not ripe for weighing conflicting interpretations, and whose one great need is a clear view of the whole. I hope that teachers who use the book will above all things attend to making their pupils seize the connexion of sense; and that to this end they will require the chapter or chapters read to be always prepared beforehand, the notes studied, and the connexion in some sort grasped by the pupil. The notes contain some words which the pupil will probably not understand, and which will have to be explained to him,— words like *nomad*, for instance, or *elliptical*. It would have been pedantic and tedious to avoid them and to use circumlocutions; but a teacher will know at a glance which they are, and will take care that the pupil is not suffered to be thrown out by them, or to get rid of the obligation to learn his lesson beforehand and to master its sense. The lesson in class will then be of double value to him: the strict preparation of the class-lesson beforehand, so universally insisted upon in our secondary schools, is an excellent discipline which our elementary schools, partly from bad habits of teaching, partly from want of books, are too much without. The seizing the connexion of sense, the apprehending *a whole*, is another discipline nearly unknown to them, and, as I have urged in the early part of this preface, most salutary. It would be possible that every child of twelve or thirteen years of age, who leaves the highest class in an elementary school, should have read this series of chapters and received a clear sense of their contents as a whole. It is not at all likely that a discipline so novel should at once be introduced on this wide scale; but could it be so, it seems to me that the fresh life and spring given to popular education would almost be such as to regenerate it. If I say this, and if I add no apologetic phrases about the faults of my own editing and

annotating, it is not that I am unconscious of their defectiveness;
but I know that the work for which they in some sort open a
way is so important as far more than to make up for it.

To make a great work pass into the popular mind is not
easy; but our series of chapters have one quality which facili-
tates this passage for them,—their boundless exhilaration. Much
good poetry is profoundly melancholy; now, the life of the
people is such that in literature they require joy. If ever that
"good time coming," for which they long, was presented with
energy and magnificence, it is in these chapters; it is impossible to
read them without catching its glow. And they present it truly
and with the true conditions; it is easy to misconceive it on a
first view, easy to misconceive its apparent conditions; but the
more these chapters sink into the mind and are apprehended,
the more manifest is their connexion with universal history, the
key they offer to it, the truth of the ideal they propose for it.
Many of us have a kind of centre-point in the far past to which
we make things converge, from which our thoughts of history
instinctively start and to which they return; it may be the
Persian War, or the Peloponnesian War, or Alexander, or the
Licinian Laws, or Cæsar. Our education is such that we are
strongly led to take this centre-point in the history of Greece or
Rome; but it may be doubted whether one who took the conquest
of Babylon and the restoration of the Jewish exiles would not have
a better. The pupil in our schools for the people, who began
with laying hold on this series of chapters as a whole, would
have a starting-point and lights of unsurpassed value for getting
a conception of the course of man's history and development as
a whole; if but for a few pupils out of many this could happen,
yet, even so, what access to a new life, almost unknown to
their class hitherto! what an extending of their horizons, what
a lifting them out of the present, what a suggestion of hope and
courage! "It is a stingy selfishness," says Barrow, "which
maketh us so sensible of crosses and so uncapable of comfort;"
there are numbers whose crosses are so many and comforts so few
that to the misery of narrow thoughts they seem almost driven
and bound; what a blessing is whatever extricates them and
makes them live with the life of the race! Our acts are, it is
most true, infinitely more important than our thoughts and

studies; but the bearing which thoughts and studies may have upon our acts is not enough considered. And the power of animation and consolation in those thoughts and studies, which, beginning by giving us a hold upon a single great work, end with giving us a hold upon the history of the human spirit, and the course drift and scope of the career of our race as a whole, cannot be over-estimated. Not pathetic only, but profound also, and of the most solid substance, was that reply made by an old Carthusian monk to the trifler who asked him how he had managed to get through his life:—"*Cogitavi dies antiquos, et annos æternos in mente habui.*"*

* Psalm lxxvii. 5.

INTRODUCTORY NOTE.

IN the year 722 B.C. the kingdom of Israel fell; its capital, Samaria, was taken by Shalmaneser king of Assyria, and its ten tribes were carried away into Assyria. Of the chosen people in the Holy Land, therefore, "there was none left but the tribe of Judah only." The great eastern empire of Assyria was then at its height of power; Media, Persia and Babylon were subject to it, and it was hoping to conquer Egypt, with which Hoshea, the last king of Israel, had made an alliance. The kingdom of Judah, also, leaned towards Egypt; for Judah, though it survived, was tributary to Assyria, and hoped by help of Egypt to break the Assyrian power. Eight years after the destruction of the kingdom of Israel, Hezekiah the king of Judah refused to pay his tribute any longer: the king of Assyria, Sennacherib, invaded Egypt and Palestine, but without success, and his army which appeared before Jerusalem was destroyed. At this time Babylon threw off the yoke of Assyria and sent an embassy to gain the friendship of Hezekiah; Media also made itself independent. Sennacherib regained his hold upon Babylon, but the end of Assyria's greatness was drawing nigh. She again lost Babylon, and in the year 625 the king of Babylon, in conjunction with the king of Media, took Niniveh and destroyed for ever the Assyrian empire. The kingdom of Media with Persia, on the one hand, and the kingdom of Babylon, on the other, were

Assyria's heirs and successors. Judah after the death of Hezekiah had no returning gleam of political prosperity. In 588, thirty-seven years after the fall of the kingdom of Assyria, and a hundred and thirty-four years after the fall of the kingdom of Israel, Nebuchadnezzar king of Babylon made a final invasion of Judah, took Jerusalem, and carried away the king and the chief part of the people to Babylon. But Nebuchadnezzar's brilliant reign founded no enduring power for Babylon. His successors became engaged in war with the Medo-Persian kingdom; and it was this kingdom which was to grow and succeed. Under Cyrus the Persian its fortunes prevailed; in 548 B.C., forty years after the fall of Jerusalem, he conquered the wealthy Lydian monarchy of Crœsus and the Greek cities on the western coast of Asia Minor; then, in the year 541, he turned upon Babylon, defended by its walls and waters. Against their enslaver and oppressor the Jewish exiles in Babylon saw uplifted the irresistible sword of God's instrument, this Persian prince, to whose religion the Babylonian idolatry was hateful; a victorious warrior, a wise and just statesman, favourable to Babylon's prisoners and victims, and disposed to restore the exiles of Judah to their own land. Assyria had fallen, Babylon was now falling; and in this supreme hour is heard the voice of God's prophets, commanded to comfort God's people, as follows:—

(*Isaiah*, 40—66.)

40 COMFORT ye, comfort ye my people, saith your God.
2   Speak ye comfortably to Jerusalem, and cry unto her that her warfare is accomplished, that her iniquity is pardoned; that she receiveth of the LORD'S hand double for all her rue.
3   A voice of one that crieth! In the wilderness prepare ye the way of the LORD, make straight in the desert a highway for our God.
4   Every valley shall be exalted, and every mountain and hill shall be made low; and the crooked shall be made straight, and the rough places plain;
5   And the glory of the LORD shall be revealed, and all flesh shall see it together: for the mouth of the LORD hath spoken it.
6   A voice said, Cry! And he said, What shall I cry?—All flesh is grass, and all the goodliness thereof is as the flower of the field:
7   The grass withereth, the flower fadeth, because the spirit of the LORD bloweth upon it: surely the people is grass.
8   The grass withereth, the flower fadeth; but the word of our God shall stand for ever.

9   O thou that bringest good tidings to Zion, get thee up into the high mountain; O thou that bringest good tidings

to Jerusalem, lift up thy voice with strength; lift it up, be not afraid; say unto the cities of Judah, Behold your God!

Behold, the Lord GOD will come with strong hand, and 10 his arm shall rule for him: behold, his reward is with him, and his recompence before him.

He shall feed his flock like a shepherd: he shall gather 11 the lambs with his arm, and carry them in his bosom, and shall gently lead those that are with young.

Who hath measured the waters in the hollow of 12 his hand, and meted out heaven with the span, and comprehended the dust of the earth in a measure, and weighed the mountains in scales, and the hills in a balance?

Who hath directed the Spirit of the LORD, or being his 13 counsellor hath taught him?

With whom took he counsel, and who instructed him, 14 and taught him in the path of judgment, and taught him knowledge, and shewed to him the way of understanding?

Behold, the nations are as a drop of a bucket, and are 15 counted as the small dust of the balance: behold, he taketh up the isles as a very little thing!

And Lebanon is not sufficient to burn, nor the beasts 16 thereof sufficient for a burnt offering.

All nations before him are as nothing; and they are 17 counted to him less than nothing, and vanity.

To whom then will ye liken God? or what likeness will 18 ye compare unto him?

The workman melteth an image, and the goldsmith 19 spreadeth it over with gold, and casteth silver chains.

He that is too poor for oblation chooseth a tree that 20 will not rot; he seeketh unto him a cunning workman to prepare an image, that shall not be moved.

Have ye not known? have ye not heard? hath it not 21 been told you from the beginning? have ye not understood from the foundations of the earth?

He that sitteth above the circle of the earth, and the 22 inhabitants thereof are as grasshoppers? that stretcheth out the heavens as a curtain, and spreadeth them out as a tent to dwell in?

That bringeth the princes to nothing? he maketh the 23 judges of the earth as vanity.

24 Yea, scarce shall they be planted, yea, scarce shall they be sown, yea, scarce shall their stock take root in the earth; and he shall blow upon them, and they shall wither, and the whirlwind shall take them away as stubble.
25 To whom then will ye liken me, or shall I be equal? saith the Holy One.
26 Lift up your eyes unto the heavens, and behold! who hath created these things? he bringeth out their host by number, he calleth them all by names; by the greatness of his might, for that he is strong in power, not one faileth.
27 Why sayest thou, O Jacob, and speakest, O Israel: My way is hid from the LORD, and my judgment is passed over from my God?
28 Hast thou not known? hast thou not heard, that the everlasting God, the LORD, the Creator of the ends of the earth, fainteth not, neither is weary? there is no searching of his understanding.
29 He giveth power to the faint, and to them that have no might he increaseth strength.
30 Even the youths shall faint and be weary, and the young men shall utterly fall:
31 But they that wait upon the LORD shall renew their strength; they shall mount up with wings as eagles; they shall run, and not be weary; and they shall walk, and not faint.

41 Keep silence before me, O islands, and let the nations renew their strength! let them come near, then let them speak; let us come near together to judgment.
2 Who raised up the righteous man from the east, called him to his foot, gave the nations before him, and made him rule over kings? he gave them as the dust to his sword, and as driven stubble to his bow.
3 He pursued them, and passed safely, even by the way that he had not gone with his feet.
4 Who hath wrought and done it? even he that called forth the generations from the beginning: I the LORD, the first, and to the last I am he.
5 Far lands saw it, and feared; the ends of the earth were afraid, draw near, and come.

They help every one his neighbour, and every one 6
saith to his brother, Be of good courage.

So the carpenter encourageth the goldsmith, and he that 7
smootheth with the hammer him that smiteth the anvil,
saying of the solder, It is good: and he fasteneth it with
nails, that it should not be moved.

But thou, Israel my servant, Jacob whom I have cho- 8
sen, the seed of Abraham my friend;

Thou whom I have taken from the ends of the earth, 9
and called thee from the extreme borders thereof, and
said unto thee, Thou art my servant; I have chosen thee,
and not cast thee away:

Fear thou not, for I am with thee! be not dismayed, 10
for I am thy God! I will strengthen thee, yea, I will help
thee, yea, I will uphold thee with the right hand of my
righteousness.

Behold, all they that were incensed against thee shall be 11
ashamed and confounded: they shall be as nothing; and
they that strive with thee shall perish.

Thou shalt seek them, and shalt not find them, even 12
them that contended with thee: they that war against
thee shall be as nothing, and as a thing of nought.

For I the Lord thy God will hold thy right hand, say- 13
ing unto thee, Fear not; I help thee!

Fear not, thou worm Jacob, and thou handful Israel! 14
I help thee, saith the Lord, and thy redeemer is the Holy
One of Israel.

Behold, I will make thee a new sharp threshing instru- 15
ment having teeth: thou shalt thresh the mountains, and
beat them small, and shalt make the hills as chaff.

Thou shalt fan them, and the wind shall carry them 16
away, and the whirlwind shall scatter them; but thou
shalt rejoice in the Lord, and shalt glory in the Holy
One of Israel.

When the poor and needy seek water, and there is none, 17
and their tongue faileth for thirst, I the Lord will hear
them, I the God of Israel will not forsake them.

I will open rivers on high places, and fountains in the 18
midst of the valleys: I will make the wilderness a pool of
water, and the dry land springs of water.

I will plant in the wilderness the cedar, the acacia tree, 19 and the myrtle, and the olive tree; I will set in the desert the cypress tree, and the pine, and the box tree together:

20 That they may see, and know, and consider, and understand together, that the hand of the LORD hath done this, and the Holy One of Israel hath created it.

21 Produce your cause, saith the LORD; bring forth your strong reasons, saith the King of Jacob.
22 Let them bring them forth, and shew us what shall happen: let them shew the former things, what they be, that we may consider them, and know the latter end of them; or declare us things for to come.
23 Shew the things that are to come hereafter, that we may know that ye are gods! yea, do good, or do evil, that we may be dismayed, and behold it together!
24 Behold, ye are of nothing, and your work of nought: an abomination is he that chooseth you.
25 I have raised up one from the north, and he shall come: from the rising of the sun, that he should call upon my name: and he shall come upon princes as upon morter, and as the potter treadeth clay.
26 Who hath declared from the beginning, that we may know? and beforetime, that we may say, He is right! yea, there is none that sheweth, yea, there is none that declareth, yea, there is none that hath heard your words.
27 I the first said to Zion, Behold, behold it! and I gave to Jerusalem one that bringeth good tidings.
28 I look, and there is no one; even among them, and there is no counsellor, that, when I should ask of them, could answer a word.
29 Behold, they are all vanity! their works are nothing: their molten images are wind and confusion.

42 Behold my servant, whom I uphold, mine elect, in whom my soul delighteth! I have put my spirit upon him: he shall declare judgment to the Gentiles.
2 He shall not strive, nor cry, nor cause his voice to be heard in the street.
3 A bruised reed shall he not break, and smoking flax shall he not quench: he shall declare judgment with truth.
4 He shall not fail nor be discouraged, until he set judgment in the earth: far lands wait for his law.

Thus saith God the LORD, he that created the heavens, 5
and stretched them out; he that spread forth the earth,
and that which cometh out of it; he that giveth breath unto
the people upon it, and spirit to them that walk therein:

I the LORD have called thee in righteousness, and will 6
hold thine hand, and will keep thee, and give thee for a
mediator of the people, for a light of the Gentiles;

To open the blind eyes, to bring out the prisoners from 7
the prison, and them that sit in darkness out of the prison
house;

I the LORD: that is my name! and my glory will I not 8
give to another, neither my praise to graven images.

Behold, the former things are come to pass, and new 9
things do I declare: before they spring forth I tell you of
them.

Sing unto the LORD a new song, and his praise from 10
the end of the earth, ye that go down to the sea and all
that is therein; the isles, and the inhabitants thereof!

Let the wilderness and the cities thereof lift up their 11
voice, the villages that Kedar doth inhabit: let the inhabitants of the rock sing, let them shout from the top of
the mountains.

Let them give glory unto the LORD, and declare his 12
praise in the islands.

The LORD shall go forth as a mighty man, he shall stir 13
up his zeal like a man of war: he shall cry, yea, roar: he
shall behave himself mightily against his enemies.

I have long time holden my peace; I have been still, 14
and refrained myself: now will I cry like a travailing woman; I will destroy and devour at once.

I will make waste mountains and hills, and parch up all 15
their herbs; and I will make the rivers dry land, and I
will dry up the pools.

And I will bring the blind by a way that they knew 16
not, I will lead them in paths that they have not known:
I will make darkness light before them, and crooked
things straight. These things will I do unto them, and
not forsake them.

They shall be turned back, they shall be greatly 17
ashamed, that trust in graven images, that say to the
molten images, Ye are our gods.

18 Hear, ye deaf; and look, ye blind, that ye may see!
19 Who is blind, but my servant? or deaf, as my messenger that I would send? who is blind as God's liegeman, and blind as the LORD's servant?
20. Seeing many things, but thou observest not; having the ears open, but he heareth not.
21 The LORD was pleased to do it for his righteousness' sake; to magnify the law, and to make it honourable.
22 But this is a people robbed and spoiled; they are all of them snared in dungeons, and they are hid in prison houses: they are for a prey, and none delivereth; for a spoil, and none saith, Restore.
23 Who among you will give ear to this? who will hearken and hear concerning the fore time?
24 Who gave Jacob for a spoil, and Israel to the robbers? did not the LORD, he against whom we have sinned? for they would not walk in his ways, neither were they obedient unto his law.
25 Therefore he hath poured upon him the fury of his anger, and the strength of battle; and it hath set him on fire round about, yet he knew not, and it burned him, yet he laid it not to heart.

43 . But now thus saith the LORD that created thee, O Jacob, and he that formed thee, O Israel! Fear not for I have redeemed thee; I have called thee by thy name, thou art mine.
2 When thou passest through the waters, I will be with thee, and through the rivers, they shall not overflow thee: when thou walkest through the fire, thou shalt not be burned, neither shall the flame kindle upon thee.
3 For I am the LORD thy God, the Holy One of Israel, thy Saviour: I give Egypt for thy ransom, Ethiopia and Saba for thee.
4 Because thou art precious in my sight, honourable, and I have loved thee, therefore will I give men for thee, and people for thy life.
5 Fear not, for I am with thee! I will bring thy seed from the east, and gather thee from the west:
6 I will say to the north, Give up! and to the south, Keep not back! bring my sons from far, and my daughters from the ends of the earth,
7 Even every one that is called by my name: for I have

created him for my glory, I have formed him, yea, I have made him.

Bring forth the blind people that have eyes, and the 8 deaf that have ears!

Let all the nations be gathered together, and let the 9 Gentiles be assembled: who among them can declare this? Or let them shew us former things: let them bring forth their witnesses, that they may be justified: let one hear, and say, It is truth!

Ye are my witnesses, saith the LORD, and my servant 10 whom I have chosen, that ye may know and believe me, and understand that I am he: before me there was no God formed, neither shall there be after me.

I, even I, am the LORD, and beside me there is no 11 saviour.

I have declared, and have saved, and I have shewed, 12 and it was no strange god that was among you: therefore ye are my witnesses, saith the LORD, that I am God.

Yea, before the day was, I am he, and there is none 13 that can take away out of my hand: I will work, and who shall let it?

Thus saith the LORD, your redeemer, the Holy One of 14 Israel: For your sake I have sent to Babylon, and do make them all to flee away, and the Chaldeans upon the ships of their pleasure;

I the LORD, your Holy One, the creator of Israel, your 15 King.

Thus saith the LORD, which maketh a way in the sea, 16 and a path in the mighty waters;

Which bringeth forth the chariot and horse, the army 17 and the power; they shall lie down together, they shall not rise: they are extinct, they are quenched as tow.

Remember not the former things, neither consider the 18 things of old.

Behold, I do a new thing! now it shall spring forth; 19 shall ye not know it? I will even make a way in the wilderness, and rivers in the desert.

The beast of the field shall honour me, the jackals and 20 the ostriches: because I give waters in the wilderness, and rivers in the desert, to give drink to my people, my chosen,

21 This people that I formed for myself; they shall shew forth my praise.
22 . But thou hast not called upon me, O Jacob! but thou hast been careless of me, O Israel!
23 . Thou hast not brought me the lambs of thy burnt offering, neither hast thou honoured me with thy sacrifices: I have not burdened thee with an offering, nor wearied thee with incense.
24 Thou hast bought me no sweet cane with money, neither hast thou filled me with the fat of thy sacrifices: but thou hast burdened me with thy sins, thou hast wearied me with thine iniquities.
25 I, even I, am he that blotteth out thy transgressions for mine own sake, and will not remember thy sins.
26 Put me in remembrance: let us plead together: declare thou, that thou mayest be justified!
27 Thy first father hath sinned, and thy teachers have transgressed against me.
28 Therefore I have profaned the princes of the sanctuary, and have given Jacob to the curse, and Israel to reproaches.

44 Yet now hear, O Jacob my servant, and Israel, whom I have chosen!
2 Thus saith the LORD that made thee, and formed thee from the womb, which will help thee: Fear not, O Jacob, my servant; and thou, Jeshurun, whom I have chosen!
3 For I will pour water upon him that is thirsty, and floods upon the dry ground: I will pour my spirit upon thy seed, and my blessing upon thine offspring:
4 And they shall spring up as the grass amidst water, as willows by the water courses.
5 One shall say, I am the LORD'S, and another shall call himself by the name of Jacob, and another shall subscribe with his hand unto the LORD, and surname himself by the name of Israel.
6 Thus saith the LORD the king of Israel, and his redeemer the LORD of hosts: I am the first, and I am the last; and beside me there is no God.
7 And who, as I, hath foretold (let him declare it, and set it in order for me!) since I appointed the ancient people? and the things that are coming, and shall come, let them shew!
8 Fear ye not, neither be afraid: have not I told thee

from aforetime, and have declared it? ye are even my witnesses. Is there a God beside me? yea, there is no God; I know not any.

They that make a graven image are all of them vanity, 9 and their delectable things shall not profit: and they are their own witnesses, they see not, nor know, that they may be ashamed.

Who hath formed a god, or molten an image that is 10 profitable for nothing?

Behold, all his fellows shall be ashamed, and the work- 11 men, that are but men. Let them all be gathered together, let them stand up; they shall fear, they shall be ashamed together.

The smith with the tongs both worketh in the coals, 12 and fashioneth it with hammers, and worketh it with the strength of his arms: yea, he is hungry, and his strength faileth: he drinketh no water, and is faint.

The carpenter stretcheth out his rule; he marketh it 13 out with a line; he fitteth it with planes, and he marketh it out with the compass, and maketh it after the figure of a man, according to the beauty of a man; that it may remain in the house.

He heweth him down cedars, and taketh the cypress 14 and the oak: he chooseth for himself among the trees of the forest: he planteth an ash, and the rain doth nourish it.

Then shall it be for a man to burn, for he will take 15 thereof, and warm himself; yea, he kindleth it, and baketh bread; yea, he maketh a god, and worshippeth it; he maketh it a graven image, and falleth down thereto.

He burneth part thereof in the fire; with part thereof 16 he eateth flesh; he roasteth roast, and is satisfied: yea, he warmeth himself, and saith, Aha, I am warm, I have seen the fire!

And the residue thereof he maketh a god, even his 17 graven image: he falleth down unto it, and worshippeth it, and prayeth unto it, and saith: Deliver me, for thou art my god!

They have not known nor understood; for he hath 18 shut their eyes, that they cannot see, and their hearts, that they cannot understand.

And none considereth in his heart, neither is there 19

knowledge nor understanding to say: I have burned part of it in the fire, yea, also I have baked bread upon the coals thereof, I have roasted flesh, and eaten it; and shall I make the residue thereof an abomination? shall I fall down to the stock of a tree?

20 He feedeth on ashes: a deceived heart hath turned him aside, that he cannot deliver his soul, nor say: Is there not a lie in my right hand?

21 Remember this, O Jacob and Israel, for thou art my servant! I have formed thee, thou art my servant: O Israel, thou shalt not be forgotten of me!

22 I have blotted out, as a thick cloud, thy transgressions, and, as a cloud, thy sins: return unto me, for I have redeemed thee.

23 Sing, O ye heavens, for the LORD hath done it: shout, ye foundations of the earth: break forth into singing, ye mountains, O forest, and every tree therein! for the LORD hath redeemed Jacob, and glorified himself in Israel.

24 Thus saith the LORD, thy redeemer, and he that formed thee from the womb, I the LORD that maketh all things, that stretcheth forth the heavens alone, that spreadeth abroad the earth by myself;

25 That frustrateth the tokens of the liars, and maketh diviners mad; that turneth wise men backward, and maketh their knowledge foolish;

26 That confirmeth his word to his servant, and performeth his counsel toward his messengers; that saith to Jerusalem, Thou shalt be inhabited! and to the cities of Judah, Ye shall be built, and I will raise up the decayed places thereof!

27 That saith to the deep, Be dry, and I will dry up thy rivers!

28 That saith of Cyrus, He is my shepherd, and shall perform all my pleasure, even saying to Jerusalem, Thou shalt be built, and to the temple, Thy foundation shall be laid!

45 Thus saith the LORD to his anointed, to Cyrus, whose right hand I have holden, to subdue nations before him; and I will ungird the loins of kings, to open before him the two leaved gates, and the gates shall not be shut;

2 I will go before thee, and make the crooked places straight: I will break in pieces the gates of brass, and cut in sunder the bars of iron:

3 And I will give thee the treasures hid in darkness, and concealed riches of secret places, that thou mayest know that I am the LORD which call thee by thy name, the God of Israel.

4 For Jacob my servant's sake, and Israel mine elect, I have even called thee by thy name: I have surnamed thee, though thou hast not known me.

5 I am the LORD, and there is none else, there is no God beside me: I girded thee, though thou hast not known me:

6 That they may know from the rising of the sun, and from the west, that there is none beside me: I am the LORD, and there is none else.

7 I form the light, and create darkness: I make peace, and create evil: I the LORD do all these things.

8 Drop down, ye heavens, from above, and let the skies pour down righteousness! let the earth open, and bring forth salvation, and let righteousness spring up together! I the LORD have created it.

9 Woe unto him that striveth with his Maker! Let the potsherd strive with the potsherds of the earth. Shall the clay say to him that fashioneth it, What makest thou? or thy work, He hath no hands?

10 Woe unto him that saith unto his father, What begettest thou? or to his mother, What hast thou brought forth?

11 Thus saith the LORD, the Holy One of Israel and his Maker: Ask ye me of things to come concerning my sons? and concerning the work of my hands command ye me?

12 I have made the earth, and created man upon it: I, even my hands, have stretched out the heavens, and all their host have I commanded.

13 I have raised him up in righteousness, and I will direct all his ways: he shall build my city, and he shall let go my captives, not for price nor reward, saith the LORD of hosts.

14 Thus saith the LORD, The labour of Egypt, and merchandise of Ethiopia and of the Sabeans, men of stature, shall come over unto thee, and they shall be thine: they

shall come after thee; in chains they shall come over, and they shall fall down unto thee, they shall make supplication unto thee, saying, Surely God is in thee, and there is none else, there is no God!

15 ·Verily thou art a God whose way is hidden, O God of Israel, the Saviour!

16 They shall be ashamed, and also confounded, all of them, they shall go to confusion together that are makers of idols.

17 But Israel shall be saved in the LORD with an everlasting salvation: ye shall not be ashamed nor confounded world without end.

18 For thus saith the LORD that created the heavens, God himself that formed the earth and made it; he hath established it, he created it not in vain, he formed it to be inhabited; I the LORD, and there is none else:

19 I have not spoken in secret, in a dark place of the earth: I said not unto the seed of Jacob, Seek ye me in vain! I the LORD speak uprightly, I declare things that are right.

20 Assemble yourselves and come, draw near together, ye that are escaped of the nations! they have no knowledge that set up the wood of their graven image, and pray unto a god that cannot save.

21 Tell ye, and bring them near, yea, let them take counsel together! who hath declared this from ancient time? who hath told it from that time? have not I the LORD? and there is no God else beside me; a just God and a Saviour; there is none beside me.

22 Look unto me, and be ye saved, all the ends of the earth! for I am God, and there is none else.

23 I have sworn by myself, the word is gone out of my mouth in righteousness, and shall not return, that unto me every knee shall bow, every tongue shall swear.

24 Surely, shall one say, in the LORD have I righteousness and strength! Even to him shall men come, and all that are incensed against him shall be ashamed.

25 In the LORD shall all the seed of Israel be justified, and shall glory.

6 Bel boweth down, Nebo stoopeth, their idols are upon the beasts, and upon the cattle: they are borne that ye carried; they are a burden to the weary beast.

2 They stoop, they bow down together; they cannot deliver the burden, but themselves are gone into captivity.

3 Hearken unto me, O house of Jacob, and all the remnant of the house of Israel, which are borne by me from the birth, which are carried from the womb!

4 And even to your old age I am he, and even to hoar hairs will I carry you: I have made, and I will bear; even I will carry, and will deliver you.

5 To whom will ye liken me, and make me equal, and compare me, that we may be like?

6 They lavish gold out of the bag, and weigh silver in the balance, and hire a goldsmith, and he maketh it a god: they fall down, yea, they worship.

7 They bear him upon the shoulder, they carry him, and set him in his place, and he standeth; from his place shall he not remove: yea, one shall cry unto him, yet can he not answer, nor save him out of his trouble.

8 Remember this, and shew yourselves men! bring it again to mind, O ye transgressors!

9 Remember the former things of old: for I am God, and there is none else; I am God, and there is none like me;

10 Declaring the end from the beginning, and from ancient times the things that are not yet done, saying, My counsel shall stand, and I will do all my pleasure:

11 Calling the eagle from the east, the man that executeth my counsel from a far country: yea, I have spoken it, I will also bring it to pass; I have purposed it, I will also do it.

12 Hearken unto me, ye obdurate, that are far from righteousness!

13 I bring near my righteousness; it shall not be far off, and my salvation shall not tarry; and I will give salvation to Zion; to Israel, my glory.

47 Come down, and sit in the dust, O virgin daughter of Babylon, sit on the ground! there is no throne, O daughter of the Chaldeans! for thou shalt no more be called tender and delicate.

2 Take the millstones, and grind meal: uncover thy locks, make bare the leg, uncover the thigh, pass over the rivers.

3 Thy nakedness shall be uncovered, yea, thy shame shall

be seen : I will take vengeance, and I will be entreated of for thee by no man.

4 As for our redeemer, the LORD of hosts is his name, the Holy One of Israel.

5 Sit thou silent, and get thee into darkness, O daughter of the Chaldeans ! for thou shalt no more be called, The lady of kingdoms.

6 I was wroth with my people, I polluted mine inheritance, and gave them into thine hand : thou didst shew them no mercy; upon the ancient hast thou very heavily laid thy yoke.

7 And thou saidst, I shall be a lady for ever : so that thou didst not lay these things to thy heart, neither didst remember the latter end of it.

8 Therefore hear now this, thou that art given to pleasures, that dwellest carelessly, that sayest in thine heart, I am, and none else beside me ; I shall not sit as a widow, neither shall I know the loss of children.

9 But these two things shall come to thee in a moment in one day, the loss of children, and widowhood : they shall come upon thee in their perfection for the multitude of thy sorceries, and for the great abundance of thine enchantments.

10 For thou hast trusted in thy wickedness, thou hast said, None seeth me ! Thy wisdom and thy knowledge, it hath perverted thee; and thou hast said in thine heart, I am, and none else beside me.

11 Therefore shall evil come upon thee, thou shalt not know from whence it riseth ; and mischief shall fall upon thee, thou shalt not be able to put it off; and desolation shall come upon thee suddenly, which thou shalt not know.

12 Stand now with thine enchantments, and with the multitude of thy sorceries, wherein thou hast laboured from thy youth ! if so be thou shalt be able to profit, if so be thou mayest prevail.

13 Thou art wearied in the multitude of thy counsels ! Let now the astrologers, the stargazers, the prognosticators by the new moon, stand up, and save thee from these things that shall come upon thee.

14 Behold, they shall be as stubble! the fire shall burn them, they shall not deliver themselves from the power of

the flame! it shall not be a coal to warm at, nor a fire for a man to sit before it.

Thus shall they be unto thee with whom thou hast 15 laboured, even they with whom thou hast dealt from thy youth: they shall wander every one to his quarter; none shall save thee.

Hear ye this, O house of Jacob, which are called by **48** the name of Israel, and are come forth out of the fountain of Judah! which swear by the name of the LORD, and make mention of the God of Israel, but not in truth, nor in righteousness!

For they call themselves of the holy city, and stay them- 2 selves upon the God of Israel; the LORD of hosts is his name.

I have declared the former things from the beginning, 3 and they went forth out of my mouth, and I shewed them; I did them suddenly, and they came to pass.

Because I knew that thou art obstinate, and thy neck is 4 an iron sinew, and thy brow brass,

I have even from the beginning declared it to thee: 5 before it came to pass I shewed it thee: lest thou shouldest say, Mine idol hath done them, and my graven image, and my molten image, hath commanded them.

Thou hast heard—see all this! and will not ye declare 6 it? I shew thee new things from this time, even hidden things, and thou didst not know them.

They are created now, and not in the former time; 7 even before this day thou heardest them not; lest thou shouldest say, Behold, I knew them.

Yea, thou heardest not, yea, thou knewest not, yea, 8 beforehand thine ear was not opened; for I knew that thou wouldest deal very treacherously, and wast called a transgressor from the womb.

For my name's sake will I defer mine anger, and for my 9 praise will I refrain for thee, that I cut thee not off.

Behold, I have refined thee, but not gotten therefrom 10 silver; I have tried thee in the furnace of affliction.

For mine own sake, even for mine own sake, will I do 11 it. for how should my name be polluted? and I will not give my glory unto another.

Hearken unto me, O Jacob and Israel, my called! I am 12 he; I am the first, I also am the last.

13 Mine hand also hath laid the foundation of the earth, and my right hand hath spread out the heavens: when I call unto them, they stand forth together.

14 All ye, assemble yourselves, and hear: which among them hath declared these things? The man whom the LORD loveth will do his pleasure on Babylon, and his chastisement on the Chaldeans.

15 I, even I, have spoken; yea, I have called him: I have brought him, and he shall make his way prosperous.

16 Come ye near unto me, hear ye this: I have not spoken in secret from the beginning; from the time that it was, there am I. (And now the Lord GOD, and his Spirit, hath sent me.)

17 Thus saith the LORD, thy Redeemer, the Holy One of Israel: I am the LORD thy God which teacheth thee to profit, which leadeth thee by the way that thou shouldest go

18 O that thou hadst hearkened to my commandments! then had thy peace been as a river, and thy righteousness as the waves of the sea:

19 Thy seed also had been as the sand, and the offspring of thy bowels like the grains thereof; his name should not have been cut off nor destroyed from before me.

20 Go ye forth of Babylon, flee ye from the Chaldeans, with a voice of singing declare ye, tell this, utter it even to the end of the earth! say ye: The LORD hath redeemed his servant Jacob,

21 And they thirsted not when he led them through the deserts; he caused the waters to flow out of the rock for them; he clave the rock also, and the waters gushed out.

22 No peace, saith the LORD, unto the wicked!

49 LISTEN, O isles, unto me; and hearken, ye people, from far; The LORD hath called me from the womb: from the bowels of my mother hath he made mention of my name.

2 And he hath made my mouth like a sharp sword; in the shadow of his hand hath he hid me, and made me a polished shaft; in his quiver hath he hid me;

3 And said unto me, Thou art my servant, O Israel, in whom I will be glorified.

Then I said: I have laboured in vain, I have spent my 4
strength for nought, and in vain ; yet surely my righteousness is with the LORD, and my recompence with my God.

And now, saith the LORD that formed me from the womb 5
to be his servant, to bring Jacob again to him, and that
Israel may be gathered ; (for I have honour in the eyes
of the LORD, and my God is my strength ;)

And he said: It is a light thing that thou shouldest be 6
my servant to raise up the tribes of Jacob, and to restore the preserved of Israel; I will also give thee for a
light to the Gentiles, that my salvation may be unto the
end of the earth.

Thus saith the LORD, the Redeemer of Israel, his 7
Holy One, to him whom man despiseth, to him whom
the people abhorreth, to a servant of tyrants : Kings shall
see and arise, princes also shall worship, because of the
LORD that is faithful, the Holy One of Israel, and he
chose thee.

Thus saith the LORD: In an acceptable time have I 8
heard thee, and in a day of salvation have I helped thee;
and I will preserve thee, and give thee for a mediator of
the people, to establish the land, to cause to inherit the
desolate heritages ;

That thou mayest say to the prisoners, Go forth! to 9
them that are in darkness, Shew yourselves! They shall
feed in the ways, and their pastures shall be in all high
places.

They shall not hunger nor thirst, neither shall the heat 10
nor sun smite them; for he that hath mercy on them
shall lead them, even by the springs of water shall he
guide them.

And I will make all my mountains a way, and my high- 11
ways shall be cast up.

Behold, these shall come from far ; and, lo, these from 12
the north and from the west; and these from the land of
Sinim.

Sing, O heavens, and be joyful, O earth, and break 13
forth into singing, O mountains! for the LORD hath comforted his people, and doth have mercy upon his afflicted.

But Zion said, The LORD hath forsaken me, and my 14
Lord hath forgotten me!

Can a woman forget her sucking child, that she should 15

not have compassion on the son of her womb? yea, they may forget, yet will I not forget thee.

16 Behold, I have graven thee upon the palms of my hands; thy walls are continually before me.
17 Thy children shall make haste; thy destroyers and they that made thee waste shall go forth of thee.
18 Lift up thine eyes round about, and behold! all these gather themselves together, and come to thee. As I live, saith the Lord, thou shalt surely clothe thee with them all, as with an ornament, and bind them on thee, as a bride doeth.
19 For thy waste and thy desolate places, and the land of thy destruction, shall even now be too narrow by reason of the inhabitants, and they that swallowed thee up shall be far away.
20 The children which thou shalt have, after thou hast lost the other, shall say again in thine ears, The place is too strait for me; give place to me that I may dwell.
21 Then shalt thou say in thine heart: Who hath begotten me these, seeing I have lost my children, and am desolate, a captive, and removing to and fro? and who hath brought up these? Behold, I was left alone; these, where had they been?
22 Thus saith the Lord God: Behold, I will lift up mine hand to the Gentiles, and set up my standard to the people; and they shall bring thy sons in their arms, and thy daughters shall be carried upon their shoulders.
23 And kings shall be thy nursing fathers, and their queens thy nursing mothers: they shall bow down to thee with their face toward the earth, and lick up the dust of thy feet; and thou shalt know that I am the Lord; for they shall not be ashamed that wait for me.
24 Shall the prey be taken from the mighty, or the captivity of the righteous be loosed?
25 But thus saith the Lord: Even the captives of the mighty shall be taken away, and the prey of the terrible shall be loosed: for I will contend with him that contendeth with thee, and I will save thy children.
26 And I will feed them that oppress thee with their own flesh, and they shall be drunken with their own blood, as with new wine; and all flesh shall know that I the Lord am thy Saviour, and thy Redeemer the mighty One of Jacob.

50 Thus saith the LORD, Where is the bill of your mother's divorcement, whom I have put away? or which of my creditors is it to whom I have sold you? Behold, for your iniquities have ye sold yourselves, and for your transgressions is your mother put away.

2 Wherefore, when I came, was there no man? when I called, was there none to answer? Is my hand shortened at all, that it cannot redeem? or have I no power to deliver? behold, at my rebuke I dry up the sea, I make the rivers a wilderness: their fish stinketh, because there is no water, and dieth for thirst.

3 I clothe the heavens with blackness, and I make sackcloth their covering.

4 The Lord GOD hath given me the tongue of the learned, that I should know how to speak a word in season to him that is weary: he wakeneth morning by morning, he wakeneth mine ear to hear as the learned.

5 The Lord GOD hath opened mine ear, and I was not rebellious, neither turned away back.

6 I gave my back to the smiters, and my cheeks to them that plucked off the hair: I hid not my face from shame and spitting.

7 For the Lord GOD will help me, therefore shall I not be confounded; therefore have I set my face like a flint, and I know that I shall not be ashamed.

8 He is near that justifieth me; who will contend with me? let us stand together! who is mine adversary? let him come near to me!

9 Behold, the Lord GOD will help me; who is he that shall condemn me? lo, they all shall wax old as a garment, the moth shall eat them up.

10 Who is among you that feareth the LORD? let him obey the voice of his servant! that walketh in darkness, and hath no light? let him trust in the name of the LORD, and stay upon his God!

11 Behold, all ye that kindle a fire, that compass yourselves about with burning darts: get ye into the flame of your fire, and among the darts that ye have kindled! This shall ye have of mine hand; ye shall lie down in sorrow.

51 Hearken to me, ye that follow after righteousness, ye that seek the LORD! look unto the rock whence ye are hewn, and to the hole of the pit whence ye are digged.

2 Look unto Abraham your father, and unto Sarah that bare you; for I called him when he was alone, and blessed him, and increased him.

3 For the LORD shall comfort Zion, he will comfort all her waste places, and he will make her wilderness like Eden, and her desert like the garden of the LORD; joy and gladness shall be found therein, thanksgiving, and the voice of melody.

4 Hearken unto me, my people, and give ear unto me, O my nation! for a law shall proceed from me, and I will make my judgment to rest for a light of the Gentiles.

5 My righteousness is near, my salvation is gone forth, and mine arms shall judge the people; far lands shall wait upon me, and on mine arm shall they trust.

6 Lift up your eyes to the heavens, and look upon the earth beneath! for the heavens shall vanish away like smoke, and the earth shall wax old like a garment, and they that dwell therein shall die in like manner; but my salvation shall be for ever, and my righteousness shall not be abolished.

7 Hearken unto me, ye that know righteousness, the people in whose heart is my law! fear ye not the reproach of men, neither be ye afraid of their revilings.

8 For the moth shall eat them up like a garment, and the worm shall eat them like wool; but my righteousness shall be for ever, and my salvation from generation to generation.

9 Awake, awake, put on strength, O arm of the LORD! awake, as in the ancient days, in the generations of old. Art thou not it that hath cut Rahab, and wounded the dragon?

10 Art thou not it which hath dried the sea, the waters of the great deep? that hath made the depths of the sea a way for the ransomed to pass over?

11 Even so the redeemed of the LORD shall return, and come with singing unto Zion, and everlasting joy shall be upon their head: they shall obtain gladness and joy, and sorrow and mourning shall flee away.

12 I, even I, am he that comforteth you! who art thou,

that thou shouldest be afraid of a man that shall die, and of the son of man which shall be made as grass;

And forgettest the LORD thy maker, that hath stretched 13 forth the heavens, and laid the foundations of the earth; and hast feared continually every day because of the fury of the oppressor, as if he were ready to destroy? and where is the fury of the oppressor?

The captive exile shall very soon be loosed; he shall 14 not die in the pit, neither shall his bread fail.

For I am the LORD thy God, that divided the sea, 15 whose waves roared: The LORD of hosts is his name.

And I have put my words in thy mouth, and I have 16 covered thee in the shadow of mine hand, that I may plant the heavens, and lay the foundations of the earth, and say unto Zion, Thou art my people!

Awake, awake, stand up, O Jerusalem, which hast 17 drunk at the hand of the LORD the cup of his fury! thou hast drunken the dregs of the cup of trembling, and wrung them out.

None to guide her among all the sons whom she hath 18 brought forth! neither any to take her by the hand of all the sons that she hath brought up!

These two things are come unto thee—who shall be 19 sorry for thee? desolation with destruction, and famine with the sword: by whom shall I comfort thee?

Thy sons have fainted, they lie at all corners of the 20 streets, as a wild bull in a net: they are full of the fury of the LORD, the rebuke of thy God.

Therefore hear now this, thou afflicted, and drunken, 21 but not with wine!

Thus saith thy Lord the LORD, and thy God that 22 pleadeth the cause of his people: Behold, I have taken out of thine hand the cup of trembling, even the dregs of the cup of my fury; thou shalt no more drink it again:

But I will put it into the hand of them that afflict thee, 23 which have said to thy soul, Bow down, that we may go over! and thou hast laid thy body as the ground, and as the street, to them that went over.

Awake, awake, put on thy strength, O Zion! put on **52** thy beautiful garments, O Jerusalem, the holy city! for henceforth there shall no more come into thee the uncircumcised and the unclean.

2 Shake thyself from the dust, arise, and sit up, O Jerusalem! loose thyself from the bands of thy neck, O captive daughter of Zion!
3 For thus saith the LORD: Ye have sold yourselves for nought, and ye shall be redeemed without money.
4 For thus saith the Lord GOD: My people went down aforetime into Egypt to sojourn there, and the Assyrian oppressed them for nought.
5 Now therefore what have I here, saith the LORD, that my people is taken away for nought? they that rule over them make them to howl, saith the LORD, and my name continually every day is blasphemed.
6 Therefore my people shall know my name: therefore they shall know in that day that I am he that doth speak: behold, it is I!
7 How beautiful upon the mountains are the feet of him that bringeth good tidings, that publisheth peace! that bringeth good tidings of good, that publisheth salvation! that saith unto Zion, Thy God reigneth!
8 Thy watchmen lift up the voice, with the voice together do they sing; for eye to eye they behold, how that the LORD doth bring again Zion.
9 Break forth into joy, sing together, ye waste places of Jerusalem! for the LORD hath comforted his people, he hath redeemed Jerusalem.
10 The LORD hath made bare his holy arm in the eyes of all the nations, and all the ends of the earth shall see the salvation of our God.
11 Depart ye, depart ye, go ye out from thence, touch no unclean thing! go ye out of the midst of her! be ye clean, that bear the vessels of the LORD!
12 For ye shall not go out with haste, nor go by flight; for the LORD will go before you, and the God of Israel will be your rereward.

13 Behold, my servant shall prosper, he shall be exalted and extolled, and be very high.
14 As many were astonied at thee—his visage was so marred more than any man, and his form more than the sons of men—
15 So shall many nations exult in him: kings shall shut

their mouths before him: for that which had not been told them shall they see, and that which they had not heard shall they consider.

53 Who believed what we heard, and to whom was the arm of the LORD revealed?

2 For he grew up before him as a slender plant, and as a root out of a dry ground: he had no form nor comeliness, and when we saw him, there was no beauty that we should desire him.

3 He was despised and rejected of men, a man of sorrows, and acquainted with grief; and we hid as it were our faces from him; he was despised, and we esteemed him not.

4 Surely he hath borne our griefs, and carried our sorrows! yet we did esteem him stricken, smitten of God, and afflicted.

5 But he was wounded for our transgressions, he was bruised for our iniquities: the chastisement of our peace was upon him, and with his stripes we are healed.

6 All we like sheep were gone astray, we were turned every one to his own way; and the LORD hath laid on him the iniquity of us all.

7 He was oppressed, and he was afflicted, yet he opened not his mouth: as a lamb is brought to the slaughter, and as a sheep before her shearers is dumb, so he opened not his mouth.

8 He was taken from prison and from judgment; and who of his generation regarded it, why he was cut off out of the land of the living? for the transgression of my people was he stricken!

9 And he made his grave with the wicked, and with sinners in his death; although he had done no violence, neither was any deceit in his mouth.

10 Yet it pleased the LORD to bruise him; he hath put him to grief;—when thou hast made his soul an offering for sin, he shall see his seed, he shall prolong his days, and the pleasure of the LORD shall prosper in his hand.

11 He shall see of the travail of his soul, and shall be satisfied: by his knowledge shall my righteous servant justify many; for he shall bear their iniquities.

12 Therefore will I divide him his portion with the great, and he shall divide the spoil with the strong! because he

hath poured out his soul unto death; and he was numbered with the transgressors; and he bare the sin of many, and made intercession for the transgressors.

54 . Sing, O barren, thou that didst not bear! break forth into singing, and cry aloud, thou that didst not travail with child! for more are the children of the desolate than the children of the married wife, saith the LORD.

2 Enlarge the place of thy tent, and let them stretch forth the curtains of thine habitations; spare not, lengthen thy cords, and strengthen thy stakes!

3 For thou shalt break forth on the right hand and on the left; and thy seed shall inherit the Gentiles, and make the desolate cities to be inhabited.

4 Fear not, for thou shalt not be ashamed! neither be thou confounded, for thou shalt not be put to shame! for thou shalt forget the shame of thy youth, and shalt not remember the reproach of thy widowhood any more.

5 For thy Maker is thine husband, the LORD of hosts is his name: and thy Redeemer the Holy One of Israel, the God of the whole earth shall he be called.

6. For the LORD hath called thee as a woman forsaken and grieved in spirit, and a wife of youth, when thou wast refused, saith thy God.

7 For a small moment have I forsaken thee, but with great mercies will I gather thee.

8 In a little wrath I hid my face from thee for a moment; but with everlasting kindness will I have mercy on thee, saith the LORD thy Redeemer.

9 For this is as the waters of Noah unto me; for as I have sworn that the waters of Noah should no more go over the earth, so have I sworn that I would not be wroth with thee, nor rebuke thee.

10 For the mountains shall depart, and the hills be removed; but my kindness shall not depart from thee, neither shall the covenant of my peace be removed, saith the LORD that hath mercy on thee.

11 O thou afflicted, tossed with tempest, and not comforted! behold, I will lay thy stones with fair colours, and lay thy foundations with sapphires;

12 And I will make thy windows of agates, and thy gates of carbuncles, and all thy borders of pleasant stones.

And all thy children shall be taught of the Lord; and 13
great shall be the peace of thy children.

In righteousness shalt thou be established: be thou far 14
from anguish, for thou shalt not fear! and from terror, for
it shall not come near thee!

Behold, if any gather together against thee, it is not by 15
me: whosoever shall gather together against thee shall
come over unto thy part.

Behold, I have created the smith that bloweth the coals 16
in the fire, and that bringeth forth a weapon by his work;
and I have created the waster to destroy.

No weapon that is formed against thee shall prosper; 17
and every tongue that shall rise against thee in judgment
thou shalt condemn. This is the heritage of the servants
of the Lord, and their righteousness of me, saith the
Lord.

Ho, every one that thirsteth, come ye to the waters, **55**
and he that hath no money! come ye, buy, and eat! yea,
come, buy wine and milk without money and without
price!

Wherefore do ye spend money for that which is not 2
bread, and your labour for that which satisfieth not?
hearken diligently unto me, and eat ye that which is good,
and let your soul delight itself in fatness.

Incline your ear, and come unto me! hear, and your 3
soul shall live! and I will make an everlasting covenant
with you, even the sure mercies of David.

Behold, I appointed him for a lawgiver to the nations, a 4
prince and commander to the nations.

Behold, thou shalt call nations that thou knowest not, 5
and nations that knew not thee shall run unto thee because of the Lord thy God, and for the Holy One of
Israel, for he hath glorified thee.

Seek ye the Lord while he may be found, call ye upon 6
him while he is near!

Let the wicked forsake his way, and the unrighteous 7
man his thoughts; and let him return unto the Lord, and
he will have mercy upon him, and to our God, for he will
abundantly pardon!

For my thoughts are not your thoughts, neither are 8
your ways my ways, saith the Lord.

For as the heavens are higher than the earth, so are my 9

ways higher than your ways, and my thoughts than your thoughts.

10 For as the rain cometh down, and the snow from heaven, and returneth not thither, but watereth the earth, and maketh it bring forth and bud, that it may give seed to the sower, and bread to the eater:

11 So shall my word be that goeth forth out of my mouth; it shall not return unto me void, but it shall accomplish that which I please, and it shall prosper in the thing whereto I sent it.

12 For ye shall go out with joy, and be led forth with peace: the mountains and the hills shall break forth before you into singing, and all the trees of the field shall clap their hands.

13 Instead of the thorn shall come up the fir tree, and instead of the brier shall come up the myrtle tree; and it shall be to the LORD for a name, for an everlasting sign that shall not be cut off.

56 Thus saith the LORD: Keep ye judgment, and do justice! for my salvation is near to come, and my righteousness to be revealed.

2 Blessed is the man that doeth this, and the son of man that layeth hold on it! that keepeth the sabbath from polluting it, and keepeth his hand from doing any evil.

3 Neither let the son of the stranger, that hath joined himself to the LORD, speak, saying, The LORD hath utterly separated me from his people: neither let the eunuch say, Behold, I am a dry tree!

4 For thus saith the LORD unto the eunuchs that keep my sabbaths, and choose the things that please me, and take hold of my covenant:

5 Even unto them will I give in mine house and within my walls a place and a name better than of sons and of daughters; I will give them an everlasting name, that shall not be cut off.

6 Also the sons of the stranger, that join themselves to the LORD, to serve him, and to love the name of the LORD, to be his servants, every one that keepeth the sabbath from polluting it, and taketh hold of my covenant;

7 Even them will I bring to my holy mountain, and make them joyful in my house of prayer: their burnt offerings and their sacrifices shall be accepted upon mine altar; for

mine house shall be called an house of prayer for all people.

The Lord God, which gathereth the outcasts of Israel, 8 saith : Yet will I gather others to him, beside those that are gathered unto him.

All ye beasts of the field, come to devour, yea, all ye 9 beasts of the forest!

His watchmen are blind: they are all ignorant, they are 10 all dumb dogs, they cannot bark; sleeping, lying down, loving to slumber.

Yea, they are greedy dogs which can never have enough, 11 and they are shepherds that cannot understand: they all look to their own way, every one for his gain, one and all of them.

Come, say they, I will fetch wine, and we will fill our- 12 selves with strong drink; and to morrow shall be as this day, and much more abundant.

The righteous perisheth, and no man layeth it to heart; **57** and merciful men are taken away, none considering that the righteous is taken away because of the evil.

He shall enter into peace! they shall rest in their beds, 2 whoso walked in his uprightness.

But draw near hither, ye sons of the sorceress, the seed 3 of the adulterer and the whore!

Against whom do ye sport yourselves? against whom 4 make ye a wide mouth, and draw out the tongue? are ye not children of transgression, a seed of falsehood,

Enflaming yourselves with idols under every green tree, 5 slaying the children in the valleys under the clifts of the rocks?

Among the smooth stones of the valley is thy portion; 6 they, they are thy lot! even to them hast thou poured a drink offering, thou hast offered a meat offering. Should I receive comfort in these?

Upon a lofty and high mountain hast thou set thy bed: 7 even thither wentest thou up to offer sacrifice.

Behind the doors also and the posts hast thou set up thy 8 remembrance: thou hast discovered thyself to another than me, and art gone up; thou hast enlarged thy bed, and made thee a covenant with them; thou lovedst their bed where thou sawest it.

9 And thou wentest unto Moloch with ointment, and didst increase thy perfumes, and didst send thy messengers far off, and didst go down even deep into hell.
10 Thou art wearied in the greatness of thy way, yet saidst thou not, There is no hope! thou hast yet found strength in thine hand, therefore thou wast not discouraged.
11 And of whom hast thou been afraid or feared, that thou hast lied, and hast not remembered me, nor laid it to thy heart? have not I held my peace even of old, and thou fearest me not?
12 I declare thy salvation! and thy handiwork, it shall not profit thee.
13 When thou criest, let thy companies of idols deliver thee! but the wind shall carry them all away, vanity shall take them; but he that putteth his trust in me shall possess the land, and shall inherit my holy mountain.
14 Thus shall it be said: Cast ye up, cast ye up, prepare the way, take the stumblingblock out of the way of my people!
15 For thus saith the high and lofty One that inhabiteth eternity, whose name is Holy: I dwell in the high and holy place, with him also that is of a contrite and humble spirit, to revive the spirit of the humble, and to revive the heart of the contrite ones.
16 For I will not contend for ever, neither will I be always wroth; for the spirit should fail before me, and the souls which I have made.
17 For the iniquity of his covetousness was I wroth, and smote him: I hid me, and was wroth, and he went on frowardly in the way of his heart.
18 I have seen his ways, and will heal him! I will lead him also, and restore comforts unto him and to his mourners.
19 I create the fruit of the lips! Peace, peace to him that is far off, and to him that is near, saith the LORD; and I will heal him.
20 But the wicked are like the troubled sea, when it cannot rest, whose waters cast up mire and dirt.
21 No peace, saith my God, to the wicked!
58 Cry aloud, spare not, lift up thy voice like a trumpet, and shew my people their transgression, and the house of Jacob their sins!
2 Yet they seek me daily, and desire to know my ways, as

a nation that did righteousness, and forsook not the ordinance of their God: they ask of me the ordinances of judgment, they desire that God should draw nigh to them.

Wherefore have we fasted, say they, and thou seest not? 3 wherefore have we afflicted our soul, and thou takest no knowledge?—Behold, in the day of your fast ye find pleasure, and exact all your labours!

Behold, ye fast for strife and debate, and to smite with 4 the fist of wickedness! your fast this day is not a fast, to make your voice to be heard on high.

Is it such a fast that I have chosen? such a day that 5 a man doth afflict his soul? is it to bow down his head as a bulrush, and to spread sackcloth and ashes under him? wilt thou call this a fast, and an acceptable day to the LORD?

Is not this the fast that I have chosen? to loose the 6 bands of wickedness, to undo the heavy burdens, and to let the oppressed go free, and that ye break every yoke?

Is it not to deal thy bread to the hungry, and that thou 7 bring the poor that are cast out to thy house? when thou seest the naked, that thou cover him; and that thou hide not thyself from thine own flesh?

Then shall thy light break forth as the morning, and 8 thine health shall spring forth speedily, and thy righteousness shall go before thee, the glory of the LORD shall be thy rereward.

Then shalt thou call, and the LORD shall answer; thou 9 shalt cry, and he shall say, Here I am! If thou take away from the midst of thee the yoke, the putting forth of the finger, and speaking vanity;

And if thou draw out thy soul to the hungry, and satisfy 10 the afflicted soul; then shall thy light rise in obscurity, and thy darkness be as the noon day.

And the LORD shall guide thee continually, and satisfy 11 thy soul in drought, and make fat thy bones; and thou shalt be like a watered garden, and like a spring of water, whose waters fail not.

And they that shall be of thee shall build the old waste 12 places: thou shalt raise up the ruins of many generations; and thou shalt be called, The repairer of the breach, The restorer of paths to dwell in.

If thou turn away thy foot from the sabbath, from doing 13

thy pleasure on my holy day, and call the sabbath a delight, the holy of the LORD, honourable; and shalt honour him, not doing thine own ways, nor finding thine own pleasure, nor speaking thine own words;

14 Then shalt thou delight thyself in the LORD, and I will cause thee to ride upon the high places of the earth, and feed thee with the heritage of Jacob thy father; for the mouth of the LORD hath spoken it.

59 Behold, the LORD'S hand is not shortened, that it cannot save, neither his ear heavy, that it cannot hear;

2 But your iniquities have separated between you and your God, and your sins have hid his face from you, that he will not hear.

3 For your hands are defiled with blood, and your fingers with iniquity; your lips have spoken lies, your tongue hath muttered perverseness.

4 None calleth for justice, nor any pleadeth for truth: they trust in vanity, and speak lies; they conceive mischief, and bring forth iniquity.

5 They hatch cockatrice' eggs, and weave the spider's web: he that eateth of their eggs dieth, and that which is crushed breaketh out into a viper.

6 Their webs shall not become garments, neither shall they cover themselves with their works: their works are works of iniquity, and the act of violence is in their hands.

7 Their feet run to evil, and they make haste to shed innocent blood: their thoughts are thoughts of iniquity; wasting and destruction are in their paths.

8 The way of peace they know not, and there is no right in their goings: they have made them crooked paths; whosoever goeth therein shall not know peace.

9 Therefore is judgment far from us, neither doth justice overtake us: we wait for light, but behold obscurity; for brightness, but we walk in darkness.

10 We grope for the wall like the blind, and we grope as if we had no eyes: we stumble at noon day as in the night; we are in desolate places as dead men.

11 We roar all like bears, and moan sore like doves: we look for judgment, but there is none; for salvation, but it is far off from us.

12 For our transgressions are multiplied before thee, and

our sins testify against us; for our transgressions are with us, and as for our iniquities, we know them;

13 In transgressing and lying against the LORD, and departing away from our God, speaking oppression and revolt, conceiving and uttering from the heart words of falsehood.

14 And justice is turned away backward, and righteousness standeth afar off; for truth is fallen in the street, and equity cannot enter.

15 Yea, truth faileth! and he that departeth from evil maketh himself a prey.

And the LORD saw it, and it displeased him that there was no judgment.

16 And he saw that there was no man, and wondered that there was no intercessor; therefore his arm brought salvation unto him, and his righteousness, it sustained him.

17 For he put on righteousness as a breastplate, and an helmet of salvation upon his head; and he put on the garments of vengeance for clothing, and was clad with zeal as a cloke.

18 According to their deeds, accordingly he will repay; fury to his adversaries, recompence to his enemies; to the far lands he will repay recompence.

19 So shall they fear the name of the LORD from the west, and his glory from the rising of the sun, when the enemy shall come in like a flood, whom the Spirit of the LORD shall drive.

20 And a redeemer shall come to Zion, and unto them that turn from transgression in Jacob, saith the LORD.

21 As for me, this is my covenant with them, saith the LORD: My spirit that is upon thee, and my words which I have put in thy mouth, shall not depart out of thy mouth, nor out of the mouth of thy seed, nor out of the mouth of thy seed's seed, saith the LORD, from henceforth and for ever.

60 Arise, shine, for thy light is come, and the glory of the LORD is risen upon thee!

2 For, behold, the darkness shall cover the earth, and gross darkness the nations! but the LORD shall arise upon thee, and his glory shall be seen upon thee.

3   And the Gentiles shall come to thy light, and kings to the brightness of thy rising.
4   Lift up thine eyes round about, and see! all they gather themselves together, they come to thee: thy sons shall come from far, and thy daughters shall be carried upon the arm.
5   Then thou shalt see and rejoice, and thine heart shall flutter and be enlarged; because the abundance of the sea shall be converted unto thee, the treasures of the Gentiles shall come unto thee.
6   The multitude of camels shall cover thee, the dromedaries of Midian and Ephah; all they from Sheba shall come, they shall bring gold and incense; and they shall shew forth the praises of the LORD.
7   All the flocks of Kedar shall be gathered together unto thee, the rams of Nebaioth shall minister unto thee: they shall come up with acceptance on mine altar, and I will glorify the house of my glory.
8   —Who are these that fly as a cloud, and as the doves to their windows?
9   Surely the isles do wait upon me, and the ships of Tarshish in front, to bring thy sons from far, their silver and their gold with them, for the name of the LORD thy God, and for the Holy One of Israel, because he hath glorified thee!
10 And the sons of strangers shall build up thy walls, and their kings shall minister unto thee; for in my wrath I smote thee, but in my favour have I had mercy on thee.
11 Therefore thy gates shall be open continually, they shall not be shut day nor night; that men may bring unto thee the treasures of the Gentiles, and that their kings may be brought.
12 For the nation and kingdom that will not serve thee shall perish; yea, those nations shall be utterly wasted.
13 The glory of Lebanon shall come unto thee, the cypress tree, the pine tree, and the box together, to beautify the place of my sanctuary; and I will make the place of my feet glorious.
14 The sons also of them that afflicted thee shall come bending unto thee; and all they that despised thee shall bow themselves down at the soles of thy feet; and they

shall call thee, The city of the LORD, the Zion of the Holy One of Israel.

Whereas thou hast been forsaken and hated, so that no 15 man went through thee, I will make thee an eternal excellency, a joy of many generations.

Thou shalt also suck the milk of the Gentiles, and shalt 16 suck the breast of kings; and thou shalt know that I the LORD am thy Saviour, and thy Redeemer the mighty One of Jacob.

For brass I will bring gold, and for iron I will bring 17 silver, and for wood brass, and for stones iron: I will also make thy officers peace, and thine exactors righteousness.

Violence shall no more be heard in thy land, wasting 18 nor destruction within thy borders; but thou shalt call thy walls Salvation, and thy gates Praise.

The sun shall be no more thy light by day, neither for 19 brightness shall the moon give light unto thee; but the LORD shall be unto thee an everlasting light, and thy God thy glory.

Thy sun shall no more go down, neither shall thy 20 moon withdraw itself; for the LORD shall be thine everlasting light, and the days of thy mourning shall be ended.

Thy people also shall be all righteous: they shall in- 21 herit the land for ever; the branch of my planting, the work of my hands, that I may be glorified.

A little one shall become a thousand, and a small one 22 a strong nation: I the LORD will hasten it in his time.

THE Spirit of the Lord GOD is upon me; because 61 the LORD hath anointed me to preach good tidings unto the afflicted; he hath sent me to bind up the brokenhearted, to proclaim liberty to the captives, and the opening of the prison to them that are bound;

To proclaim the acceptable year of the LORD, and the 2 day of vengeance of our God; to comfort all that mourn;

To appoint, unto them that mourn in Zion, to give 3 unto them beauty for ashes, the oil of joy for mourning, the garment of praise for the spirit of heaviness; that they might be called trees of righteousness, the planting of the LORD, that he might be glorified,

4 And they shall build the old wastes, they shall raise up the former desolations, and they shall repair the waste cities, the desolations of many generations.

5 And strangers shall stand and feed your flocks, and the sons of the alien shall be your plowmen and your vinedressers.

6 But ye shall be named the Priests of the LORD: men shall call you the Ministers of our God: ye shall eat the riches of the Gentiles, and in their glory shall ye boast yourselves.

7 For your shame ye shall have double; and for confusion shall my people rejoice in their portion: therefore in their land they shall possess the double; everlasting joy shall be unto them.

8 For I the LORD love judgment, I hate robbery and wrong; and I will give them their reward in truth, and I will make an everlasting covenant with them.

9 And their seed shall be known among the Gentiles, and their offspring among the people: all that see them shall acknowledge them, that they are the seed which the LORD hath blessed.

10 I will greatly rejoice in the LORD, my soul shall be joyful in my God; for he hath clothed me with the garments of salvation, he hath covered me with the robe of righteousness, as a bridegroom decketh himself with ornaments, and as a bride adorneth herself with her jewels.

11 For as the earth bringeth forth her bud, and as the garden causeth the things that are sown in it to spring forth; so the Lord GOD will cause righteousness and praise to spring forth before all the nations.

62 For Zion's sake will I not hold my peace, and for Jerusalem's sake I will not rest, until the righteousness thereof go forth as brightness, and the salvation thereof as a lamp that burneth.

2 And the Gentiles shall see thy righteousness, and all kings thy glory; and thou shalt be called by a new name, which the mouth of the LORD shall name.

3 Thou shalt also be a crown of glory in the hand of the LORD, and a royal diadem in the hand of thy God.

4 Thou shalt no more be termed Forsaken, neither shall thy land any more be termed Desolate; but thou shalt be

called My delight is in her, and thy land Married; for the LORD delighteth in thee, and thy land shall be married.

For as a young man marrieth a virgin, so shall thy sons 5 marry thee; and as the bridegroom rejoiceth over the bride, so shall thy God rejoice over thee.

—'I have set watchmen upon thy walls, O Jerusalem, which 6 shall never hold their peace day nor night.'—Ye that are the LORD'S remembrancers, keep not silence,

And give him no rest, till he establish, and till he make 7 Jerusalem a praise in the earth!

The LORD hath sworn by his right hand, and by the 8 arm of his strength: Surely I will no more give thy corn to be meat for thine enemies, and the sons of the stranger shall not drink thy wine for the which thou hast laboured;

But they that have harvested it shall eat it, and praise 9 the LORD; and they that have gathered thy wine shall drink it in the courts of my holiness.

Go through, go through the gates! prepare ye the way 10 of the people! cast up, cast up the highway! gather out the stones! lift up a standard for the nations!

Behold, the LORD hath proclaimed unto the end of the 11 world: Say ye to the daughter of Zion, Behold, thy salvation cometh! behold, his reward is with him, and his recompence before him!

And they shall call them, The holy people, The re- 12 deemed of the LORD; and thou shalt be called, Sought out, A city not forsaken.

Who is this that cometh from Edom, with dyed **63** garments from Bozrah? this that is glorious in his apparel, travelling in the greatness of his strength?

—'I that speak in righteousness, mighty to save.'—

Wherefore art thou red in thine apparel, and thy gar- 2 ments like him that treadeth in the winefat?

—'I have trodden the winepress alone, and of the nations 3 there was none with me; then trod I them in mine anger, and trampled them in my fury, and their blood was sprinkled upon my garments, and I have stained all my raiment.

'For the day of vengeance is in mine heart, and the year 4 of my redeemed is come.

5   'And I looked, and there was none to help, and I wondered that there was none to uphold; therefore mine own arm brought salvation unto me, and my fury, it upheld me.
6   'And I tread down the people in mine anger, and make them drunk in my fury, and I bring down their strength to the earth.'—

7   I will mention the lovingkindnesses of the LORD, and the praises of the LORD, according to all that the LORD hath bestowed on us; and the great goodness toward the house of Israel, which he hath bestowed on them according to his mercies, and according to the multitude of his lovingkindnesses.
8   For he said, Surely they are my people, children that will not lie! so he was their Saviour.
9   In all their affliction he was afflicted, and the angel of his presence saved them: in his love and in his pity he redeemed them; and he bare them and carried them all the days of old.
10   But they rebelled, and vexed his holy Spirit; therefore he was turned to be their enemy, and he fought against them.
11   Then remembered his people the days of old, and Moses, saying: Where is he that brought them up out of the sea with the shepherd of his flock? where is he that put his holy Spirit within them?
12   That led them by the right hand of Moses with his glorious arm, dividing the water before them, to make himself an everlasting name?
13   That led them through the deep, as an horse in the desert, and they did not stumble?
14   As a beast goeth down into the valley, the Spirit of the LORD caused them to rest: so didst thou lead thy people, to make thyself a glorious name.
15   Look down from heaven, and behold from the habitation of thy holiness and of thy glory! where is thy zeal and thy strength, the sounding of thy bowels and of thy mercies toward me? are they restrained?
16   Doubtless thou art our father, though Abraham be ignorant of us, and Israel acknowledge us not! thou, O LORD, art our father! our redeemer is thy name from everlasting!

O Lord, why hast thou made us to err from thy ways, 17
and hardened our heart from thy fear? Return for thy
servants' sake, the tribes of thine inheritance!

The people of thy holiness have had possession but a 18
little while: our adversaries have trodden down thy sanctuary.

We are thine! thou never barest rule over them; they 19
were not called by thy name.

Oh that thou wouldest rend the heavens, that thou **64**
wouldest come down! that the mountains might flow down
at thy presence,

As the fire burneth the stubble, the fire causeth the 2
water to boil! to make thy name known to thine adversaries, that the nations may tremble at thy presence.

When thou didst terrible things which we looked not 3
for, thou camest down, the mountains flowed down at thy
presence.

For since the beginning of the world men have not 4
heard, nor perceived by the ear, neither hath the eye seen,
O God, beside thee, who hath prepared such things for
him that waiteth for him.

Thou meetest him that rejoiceth and worketh righteous- 5
ness, those that remember thee in thy ways.

Behold, thou art wroth (for we have sinned) with thy
people continually!—and shall we be saved?

We are all even as the unclean, and all our righteous- 6
nesses are as filthy rags; and we all have faded as a leaf,
and our iniquities, like the wind, do take us away.

And there is none that calleth upon thy name, that stir- 7
reth up himself to take hold of thee; for thou hast hid thy
face from us, and hast consumed us, because of our iniquities.

But now, O Lord, thou art our father! we are the clay, 8
and thou our potter, and we all are the work of thy hand.

Be not wroth very sore, O Lord, neither remember 9
iniquity for ever! behold, see, we beseech thee, we are all
thy people!

Thy holy cities are a wilderness, Zion is a wilderness, 10
Jerusalem a desolation.

Our holy and our beautiful house, where our fathers 11
praised thee, is burned up with fire; and all our pleasant
things are laid waste.

12 Wilt thou refrain thyself for these things, O Lord? wilt thou hold thy peace, and afflict us very sore?

65. I gave ear to them that asked not for me, I am found of them that sought me not: I said, Behold me, behold me, unto a nation that called not upon my name.

2 I have spread out my hands all the day unto a rebellious people, which walketh in a way not good, after their own thoughts;

3 A people that provoketh me to anger continually to my face; that sacrificeth in the gardens, and burneth incense upon the tiles;

4 Which remain among the graves, and lodge in the monuments; which eat swine's flesh, and broth of abominable things is in their vessels;

5 Which say, Stand by thyself, come not near to me; for I am holier than thou! These are a smoke in my nose, a fire that burneth all the day.

6 Behold, it is written before me; I will not keep silence, but will recompense, even recompense into their bosom,

7 Your iniquities, and the iniquities of your fathers together, saith the Lord, which have burned incense upon the mountains, and blasphemed me upon the hills; therefore will I measure the reward of their former work into their bosom.

8 Thus saith the Lord: As the new wine is found in the grape cluster, and one saith, Destroy it not, for a blessing is in it! so will I do for my servants' sakes, that I may not destroy them all.

9 And I will bring forth a seed out of Jacob, and out of Judah an inheritor of my mountains; and mine elect shall inherit it, and my servants shall dwell there.

10 And Sharon shall be a fold of flocks, and the valley of Achor a place for the herds to lie down in, for my people that have sought me.

11 But ye are they that forsake the Lord, that forget my holy mountain, that prepare a table for Fortune, and that furnish the drink offering unto that which destineth.

12 Therefore will I destine you to the sword, and ye shall all bow down to the slaughter; because when I called, ye did not answer, when I spake, ye did not hear, but did evil before mine eyes, and did choose that wherein I delighted not.

Therefore thus saith the Lord GOD: Behold, my servants 13 shall eat, but ye shall be hungry; behold, my servants shall drink, but ye shall be thirsty; behold, my servants shall rejoice, but ye shall be ashamed;

Behold, my servants shall sing for joy of heart, but ye 14 shall cry for sorrow of heart, and shall howl for vexation of spirit.

And ye shall leave your name for a curse unto my 15 chosen; for the Lord GOD shall slay you, and call his servants by another name;

That he who blesseth himself in the earth shall bless 16 himself in the God of truth, and he that sweareth in the earth shall swear by the God of truth; because the former troubles are forgotten, and because they are hid from mine eyes.

For, behold, I create new heavens and a new earth; and 17 the former shall not be remembered, nor come into mind.

But be ye glad and rejoice for ever in that which I 18 create; for, behold, I create Jerusalem a rejoicing, and her people a joy.

And I will rejoice in Jerusalem, and joy in my people; 19 and the voice of weeping shall be no more heard in her, nor the voice of crying.

There shall be no more thence an infant of days, nor an 20 old man that hath not filled his days: for the child shall die an hundred years old, and the sinner being an hundred years old shall be accursed.

And they shall build houses, and inhabit them; and 21 they shall plant vineyards, and eat the fruit of them.

They shall not build, and another inhabit; they shall 22 not plant, and another eat; for as the days of a tree are the days of my people, and mine elect shall long enjoy the work of their hands.

They shall not labour in vain, nor bring forth for trouble; 23 for they are the seed of the blessed of the LORD, and their offspring with them.

And it shall come to pass, that before they call, I will 24 answer; and while they are yet speaking, I will hear.

The wolf and the lamb shall feed together, and the lion 25 shall eat straw like the bullock, and dust shall be the serpent's meat. They shall not hurt nor destroy in all my holy mountain, saith the LORD.

66 Thus saith the LORD: The heaven is my throne, and the earth is my footstool; where is the house that ye build unto me, and where is the place of my rest?

2 · For all those things hath mine hand made, and all those things were, saith the LORD; but to this man will I look, even to him that is meek and of a contrite spirit, and trembleth at my word.

3 He that killeth an ox is the same that slayeth a man; he that sacrificeth a lamb, the same that cutteth a dog's throat; he that offereth an oblation, offereth swine's blood; he that burneth incense, is he that blesseth an idol. Yea, they have chosen their own ways, and their soul delighteth in their abominations.

4 I also will choose to mock them, and will bring their fears upon them; because when I called, none did answer, when I spake, they did not hear; but they did evil before mine eyes, and chose that in which I delighted not.

5 Hear the word of the LORD, ye that tremble at his word: Your brethren that hated you, that cast you out for my name's sake, said, Let the LORD be glorified, and let your joy appear! but they shall be ashamed.

6 —A voice of noise from the city, a voice from the temple, a voice of the LORD that rendereth recompence to his enemies!

7 Before she travailed, she brought forth: before her pain came, she was delivered of a man child.

8 Who hath heard such a thing? who hath seen such things? Shall a land be brought forth in one day, or shall a nation be born at once? for as soon as Zion travailed, she brought forth her children.

9 Shall I bring to the birth, and not cause to bring forth? saith the LORD; shall I cause to bring forth, and shut the womb? saith thy God.

10 Rejoice ye with Jerusalem, and be glad with her, all ye that love her! rejoice for joy with her, all ye that mourn for her!

11 That ye may suck, and be satisfied with the breasts of her consolations; that ye may milk out, and be delighted with the abundance of her glory.

12 For thus saith the LORD: Behold, I will extend peace to

her like a river, and the glory of the Gentiles like a flowing stream: then shall ye suck, ye shall be borne upon her sides, and be dandled upon her knees.

As one whom his mother comforteth, so will I comfort 13 you, and ye shall be comforted in Jerusalem.

And when ye see this, your heart shall rejoice, and your 14 bones shall flourish like an herb; and the hand of the LORD shall be known toward his servants, and his indignation toward his enemies.

For, behold, the LORD will come with fire, and with his 15 chariots like a whirlwind, to render his anger with fury, and his rebuke with flames of fire.

For by fire and by his sword will the LORD plead with 16 all flesh, and the slain of the LORD shall be many.

They that sanctify themselves, and purify themselves in 17 the gardens behind one chief in the midst, eating swine's flesh, and the abomination, and the mouse, shall be consumed together, saith the LORD.

For I know their works and their thoughts. 18

It shall come, that I will gather all nations and tongues, and they shall come, and see my glory.

And I will set a sign among them, and I will send those 19 that escape of them unto the nations, to Tarshish, Phul and Lud that draw the bow, to Tubal and Javan, to the isles afar off, that have not heard my fame, neither have seen my glory; and they shall declare my glory among the Gentiles.

And they shall bring all your brethren for an offering 20 unto the LORD out of all nations upon horses, and in chariots, and in litters, and upon mules, and upon dromedaries, to my holy mountain Jerusalem, saith the LORD, as the children of Israel bring an offering in a clean vessel into the house of the LORD.

And of them also will I take for priests and for Levites, 21 saith the LORD.

For as the new heavens and the new earth, which I will 22 make, shall remain before me, saith the LORD, so shall your seed and your name remain.

And it shall come to pass, that from one new moon to 23

another, and from one sabbath to another, shall all flesh come to worship before me, saith the LORD.

24 And they shall go forth, and look upon the carcases of the men that have transgressed against me; for their worm shall not die, neither shall their fire be quenched, and they shall be an abhorring unto all flesh.

NOTES.

CHAPTER 40.

(For the circumstances under which this Chapter opens see the Introductory Note following the Preface.

The *Greek* Version mentioned in these notes is that of the Septuagint, or Seventy, begun at Alexandria in the third century before Christ, but not completed till the following century. It is the version which we find generally used and quoted in the New Testament. The *Vulgate* is the Latin Version of St Jerome, made at the beginning of the fifth century after Christ. It is the authorised version of the Church of Rome, and up to the Reformation was the Bible of Christendom; only for the Psalms a yet earlier Latin version, made from the Greek, not the Hebrew, maintained its ground: of this version the Latin headings to the Psalms in the Prayer-Book are relics. The *Chaldaic* Version and paraphrase was formerly thought to be nearly contemporary with the Christian era, or a little anterior to it; a considerable weight of opinion now, however, seems to be in favour of assigning this version to the third and fourth centuries after Christ. In any case it possesses great interest, having been made by learned Jews, in an idiom akin to Hebrew, and which was the idiom in common use in Palestine at the Christian era. In this idiom were interpreted the Scriptures at those "readings in the Synagogue every Sabbath-day," which we find mentioned in the New Testament; and much of these old interpretations and explanations is probably incorporated in the Chaldaic paraphrase. Other versions will be mentioned in the following notes, but they do not require special remark here.)

1. *Comfort ye, comfort ye my people.*—Sometimes *my people* is erroneously taken for the nominative of address, as if the meaning were: Be comforted, my people. It is not so: the prophets are commanded to comfort the people. "Prophets, prophesy consolations," is the opening in the Chaldaic version. And in the Greek the word *priests* is supplied at the beginning of the second verse. But the right word to supply is *prophets*.

6. *And he said, What shall I cry?*—He is the prophet to whom the command to cry came. The Greek and the Vulgate have *I said;* the Arabic version supplies, as a subject to *said*, the words *He who was commanded.* But this is not necessary: the air is full of inspiration, of divine calls and prophetic voices, and the forms of expression are naturally rapid and elliptical. After a pause, it is given to the prophet what he shall cry.

9. *O thou.*—Here the opening ends, and the main subject,—Israel's restoration by the Almighty God of Israel,—is directly entered on.

15. *The isles.*—See note on verse 1 of the following chapter.

16. *And Lebanon is not sufficient to burn.*—The trees of Lebanon are not enough for wood on the fire of sacrifice.

18. *To whom then will ye liken God?*—How should the image-deities of idolatrous Babylon be compared to this almighty and unsearchable God of Israel?

20. *He that is too poor for oblation.*—Probably a contrast is intended between the costly idol of metal and the cheaper idol of wood, just as we find the two kinds of idols put side by side again at c. 44, vv. 12—17. So

blinded are these heathens, the Prophet means, that every man must have his idol; he who is too poor for oblation, who is still more, therefore, too poor to have his molten image with work of silver and gold, will yet have his image of wood.

23. *That bringeth the princes to nothing.*—After these words, in order to complete the sense, *Have ye not known him?* should be repeated from v. 21.

26. *Their host.*—The host of the stars.

27. *Why sayest thou, O Jacob.*—How then can Jacob and Israel be faint-hearted, or despair of their restoration, when this unmatchable, all-powerful, unwearying God is their God? Compare c. 49, v. 14.

ib. My judgment is passed over.—Is neglected. My God neglects (Israel is supposed to say) to judge my cause and to give sentence for me.

CHAPTER 41.

To make still clearer the contrast between the power and wisdom of the God of Israel and of the gods of the heathen, these latter are challenged to show and compare their performances beside His.

1. *O islands.*—Literally, *coast-lands*, with especial reference to the coasts and islands of the Mediterranean, and, as these were westerly to the Jews, to the west; but used also generally in the sense of *far lands, distant regions.*

ib. Renew their strength.—Collect all their force to answer me.

2. *The righteous man from the east.*—Cyrus from Persia, which is easterly both to Babylonia and to Palestine. Cyrus had the character of a mild and just prince; and Xenophon, the Greek historian, chose him for his ideal of a virtuous ruler. The Persians themselves said, according to Herodotus, that Darius was a huckster, Cambyses a master, but Cyrus a father. But it specially weighed, besides, with the Jews, that his religion, the religion of Persia, rejected and forbade idols like the religion of Israel. With this character to mark his religion, and pursuing, too, a policy favourable to the Jews, Cyrus came to be spoken of by them almost as a servant of the true God like themselves. See Ezra i. 2: "Thus saith Cyrus King of Persia, *The Lord God of heaven* hath given me all the kingdoms of the earth."

ib. Gave the nations before him.—First the kingdom of the Medes, then Lydia, the kingdom of the rich Crœsus, and the Greek cities of Asia Minor; all conquered by Cyrus before his enterprise against Babylon.

3. *Even by the way that he had not gone.*—Even in his marches through new and unknown countries Cyrus was guided prosperously to his goal, as God's instrument.

8. *But thou, Israel.*—Amid the conquest, panic, and hurried recourse of the heathens to their idols, Israel has a secure upholder and restorer in the Lord his God.

17. *When the poor and needy seek water.*—On the march of the suffering exiles through the desert between Babylon and the Holy Land, in the promised and approaching return of the Jews to their country. In these regions water is almost the first object of a man's thoughts; the Ghassanides, one of the most powerful divisions of the Arabian race, took their name from a spring of water they fell in with on their march across the desert from Arabia into Syria. God promises his people to provide water in the wilderness and on the bare highlands for them, and verdure in the desert, that their return may be made easier.

21. *Produce your cause.*—Israel having been exhorted and encouraged, the discourse turns again to the heathen and their false gods, who had been challenged to a competition with the Lord.

22. *Let them shew the former things.*—Let the gods of the heathen show what counsel and warning they have given to their dependents in

former times, and let us see whether it has been verified; or let them give some counsel and warning to them now, and let us see whether it will be verified.

23. *One from the north, and...from the rising of the sun.*—Cyrus from Persia, which is to the north and east of Babylon.

24. *Who hath declared.*—Who of the false gods can point to warnings and prophecies fulfilled, as the God of Israel can? What have they to produce like the Lord's sentence passed two hundred years ago on Assyria in its pride of power: "When the Lord hath performed his whole work upon Mount Zion and on Jerusalem, *I will punish the fruit of the stout heart of the king of Assyria, and the glory of his high looks*" (Isaiah x. 12)—and since fulfilled in Assyria's fall? What can they produce like the Lord's sentence passed seventy years ago on Babylon in its pride of power: "I will punish the king of Babylon and that nation for their iniquity, and the land of the Chaldeans, and will make it a perpetual desolation" (Jeremiah xxv. 12)—and now being fulfilled in Babylon's danger and fast approaching fall? Nothing of this kind can they produce, and they are all vanity.

27. *I gave to Jerusalem.*—Israel had prophets and true counsellors from his God, while the heathen from their false gods had none.

CHAPTER 42.

Israel, the object of this divine favour and these divine purposes, is now more closely considered, his true mode of working is declared, his blindness and shortcomings are reproved.

1. *Behold my servant, whom I uphold; mine elect.*—The Greek supplies, "*Jacob* my servant, *Israel* mine elect." The whole passage, vv. 1—4, is applied to Christ in the New Testament, St Matt. xii. 17—21; but neither the Greek version nor the Hebrew original are there closely followed. The occasion of quoting the passage is Jesus's charge to those he healed that they should not make him known, the point primarily to be illustrated being Christ's mild, silent, and uncontentious manner of working.

2. *He shall not strive.*—More literally, shall not *clamour;* shall not speak with the high, vehement voice of men who contend. God's servant shall bring to men's hearts the word of God's righteousness and salvation by a gentle, inward, and spiritual method.

3. *A bruised reed.*—Suffering and failing hearts he shall treat tenderly, and restore them by mildness, not severity.

6. *For a mediator of the people, for the light of the Gentiles.*—We are familiar with the application of this to Christ; but it is said in the first instance of the ideal Israel, immediately represented to the speaker by God's faithful prophets bent on declaring his commandments and promises, and by the pious part of the nation, persisting, in spite of their exile among an idolatrous people, in their reliance on God and in their pure worship of Him. The ideal Israel, thus conceived, was to be God's mediator with the more backward mass of the Jewish nation, and the bringer of the saving light and health of the God of Israel to the rest of mankind.

9. *The former things are come to pass.*—Such as the prophesied fall of Assyria.

ib. *And new things do I declare.*—The approaching fall of Babylon and the restoration of Israel.

10. *Sing unto the Lord.*—In the convulsions of war and change coming upon the earth God's arm was about to be shown in the overthrow of idolatrous Babylon, and in the restoration of his chosen people; hence this song of triumph.

ib. *Ye that go down to the sea, and all that is therein.*—Compare Psalm xcvi. 11: "Let the sea make a noise, and all that therein is."

11. *The wilderness and the cities thereof.*—The great expanse of desert country between Babylonia, Palestine, and Arabia, with nomad tribes

masters of it, and settlements scattered through it where there is water. Kedar is the name of an Arabian people, descended from Ishmael, lying in the north of Arabia, next to their brother race, Nebaioth, the Nabathæans. See Gen. xxv. 13.

ib. The inhabitants of the rock.—The country above spoken of is by no means one great plain of sand, but has stony regions (Arabia Petræa), hills, and rock-forts. These are often contrasted with the undefended habitations of the nomad Arabs. "We Bedouins," says one of these Arabs, in the 6th century after Christ, to the poet Imroulcays, who sought his protection, "live in the plains, and have no castles where we can make our guests safe; go to the Jew Samuel in his castle of El-Ablak." The fidelity of this Jewish lord of an Arabian rock-fort became a proverb.

12. *In the islands.*—See note to c. 41, v. 1.

15. *I will make the rivers dry land, &c.*—The great rivers of Mesopotamia, from the nature of the country through which they flow, have from the earliest times offered scope for large engineering operations, both civil and military. Mr Layard speaks thus of the ruins of a great stone-dam he found in the Tigris: "It was one of those monuments of a great people, to be found in all the rivers of Mesopotamia, which were undertaken to ensure a constant supply of water to the innumerable canals spreading like network over the surrounding country, and which, even in the days of Alexander, were looked upon as the works of an ancient nation." Engineering works for a military object, besides the operations on the Gyndes and Euphrates attributed to Cyrus, are continually mentioned. For example, Arabian writers relate how Zebba (probably the Zenobia of our histories) built two fortresses, one on the right the other on the left bank of the Euphrates, and connected them by a tunnel, which she made by damming and turning the Euphrates when its waters were low, executing a deep cutting in its bed, bricking the cutting over, and then turning the waters back again. She hoped thus to have always a sure place of refuge, but an enemy who was at war with her got the secret of the tunnel, met her at its mouth in the second fortress when she fled from the first, and slew her.

16. *And I will bring the blind, &c.*—I will bring my faint-hearted, incredulous and undiscerning people safe through the desert to their own land.

19. *Who is blind, but my servant.*—Israel, as a whole, is faint-hearted, is slow to understand God's great purposes for it, and incredulous of them, in spite of all the experience it has had of God's guidance.

20. *The Lord was pleased, &c.*—The Lord took Israel for his chosen people, in order to exalt his law, the law of righteousness, committed to Israel; Israel is conquered, despoiled and captive; how can such things befall God's chosen people? Clearly, because of Israel's sins; because, though the chosen people, Israel would not walk in God's ways. Let Israel now return to them and be saved.

CHAPTER 43.

And saved Israel shall be, the next chapter continues; his sons shall be gathered from all the regions where they are dispersed, and shall be brought with safety and victory, as of old from the bondage of Egypt, to their own land.

3. *I give Egypt for thy ransom, Ethiopia and Saba for thee.*—In the crash now begun, the new conquering power, Persia, was about to attack and overturn other powers besides Babylon. Cambyses, the son of Cyrus, conquered Egypt and invaded Ethiopia. Saba is Meroe on the Upper Nile. The Persian king was to set free the chosen people; these other peoples, given into his hand, were to be as a ransom and a substitute for the delivered Israel.

8. *Bring forth the blind people that have eyes.*—Set free my people

Israel, who have been blind to my ways but shall see them, and deaf to my word but shall hearken to it.

9. *Let all the nations.*—The heathen and their gods are again challenged as in c. 41. See note to v. 24 of that chapter.

10. *Ye are my witnesses, &c.*—Israel is here addressed, both the blind and faint-hearted mass of the nation, and the faithful and believing few.

14. *And the Chaldeans upon the ships of their pleasure.*—"I make the Chaldeans to flee upon the barks that had before served for their pleasure." The great feature of Babylon was its river, the Euphrates, with its quays, bridges, cuts, and artificial lakes; it served alike for use and pleasure.

16. *Which maketh a way in the sea.*—A remembrance of the march out of Egypt and of Pharaoh's overthrow.

20. *The beasts of the field shall honour me.*—I will provide water in the desert for my returning people on their march through it; and by this the wild creatures of the desert, which usually suffer by the drought prevailing there, shall profit.

23. *Thou hast not brought me the lambs.*—Compare Ps. l. 8: "I will not reprove thee because of thy sacrifices or for thy burnt-offerings, because they were not always before me." The sacrificial service of the temple necessarily ceased during the exile at Babylon; God has no concern for this, neither does he plague his people about it; his concern is because his people plague *him* with their sins.

24. *No sweet cane.*—A spice reed, *calamus aromaticus*, used for the holy anointing oil. See Exod. xxx. 23, where it is called "sweet calamus," and mentioned along with cinnamon.

26. *Let us plead together.*—As the heathen and their deities were challenged recently, so Israel is now challenged to try its cause with God.

27. *Thy first father.*—Jacob, by whose representative name the Jewish people is throughout addressed. See Hos. xii. 2, 3: "The Lord will punish Jacob according to his ways, according to his doings will he recompense him; he took his brother by the heel in the womb," &c. But probably a general sense is meant to be given to the expression: "thy forefathers," "thy race from its first beginning."

28. *The princes of the sanctuary.* The chief priests. See Jer. lii. 24.

CHAPTER 44.

Nevertheless Israel shall be restored, and so evidently blest that other nations shall attach themselves to him, call themselves by his name, and become servants of his God. For his God is the only God, the idols are vanity; amidst the joy of the whole earth, God will perform his promise and restore Israel by the hand of Cyrus.

2. *Jeshurun.*—Probably a diminutive of endearment, coming originally from Jashar, *upright*, and with a force something like that of *Goodchild*. The Greek has, *my beloved Israel*, the Vulgate, *rectissime*, Luther, *Frommer*, "pious one."

3. *The ancient people.*—More literally, the *everlasting* people; Israel, the chosen, eternal people of God.

7. *Let them shew.*—A challenge as at c. 41, vv. 21—24; see the notes there.

8. *They are their own witnesses.*—They themselves have the plain evidence of the nullity of their gods; but they are blind to it, that they may come to shame and ruin.

11. *That are but men.*—That are mere mortal men, and yet make gods!

12. *The smith.*—There is here mention, first, of the molten image made by the smith, and then of the cheaper wooden image made by the carpenter. See c. 40, v. 20, and the note there.

ib. Yea, he is hungry.—This god-maker is hungry and faint, even at the very time he is at his god-making!

27. *That saith to the deep, &c.*—There is reference here to the Israelites' passage of the Red Sea, and probably also to the operations of Cyrus in drying and turning the rivers of Babylon.

CHAPTER 45.

Cyrus is God's instrument, and those Jews that have difficulty in recognising him as such, are warned not to be more wise than God. God has raised up Cyrus and is directing his wars, that Israel may be saved, and that the world may be saved with Israel in Israel's God, the sole source of salvation.

1. *To his anointed, to Cyrus.*—The Vulgate keeps the Greek word for *anointed*, and has *Christo meo Cyro*.

ib. *I will ungird the loins.*—To gird the loins is to make fit for action and to fill with strength; so to *un*gird them is to make powerless for action and to leave defenceless.

ib. *To open before him the two-leaved gates, &c.*—The gates of Babylon and the other cities besieged by Cyrus.

4. *I have surnamed thee.*—"My Shepherd." See the last verse of the preceding chapter.

8. *Drop down, ye heavens, &c.*—Compare Deut. xxxii. 2: My doctrine shall drop as the rain, my speech shall distil as the dew, &c.

ib. *Have created him.*—Cyrus.

9. *Woe unto him.*—God here turns to Israel, who was looking for "a rod out of the stem of Jesse" to restore the Jews in triumph to Jerusalem, and was little prepared to accept an alien deliverer like Cyrus. "Will Israel be more wise than God who made him and the world and rules them in his own manner?" is the substance of this and the following verses.

ib. *Thy work.*—In common speech we should say, *one's* work. Shall one's work say of him that fashioneth it, &c.

11. *Ask ye me of things to come, &c.*—See note to v. 9. Will ye take the disposition of things out of my hands, and direct me how I am to deal with my own chosen people?

13. *I have raised him, &c.*—*Him* is Cyrus, *my city* is Jerusalem, *my captives* are the Jews.

14. *The labour of Egypt, &c.*—See c. 43, v. 3, and the note there. Saba, or Meroe, on the upper Nile, was the centre of a great caravan trade between Ethiopia, Egypt and North Africa, Arabia and India. Herodotus speaks (iii. 20) of the Ethiopians as "the tallest of men."

ib. *Shall come over unto thee.*—*Thee* is Israel. The conquest of strange nations by Cyrus shall acquaint these nations with Israel and Israel's God, and make them see that only in this God is salvation.

ib. *In chains.*—After their conquest by Cyrus.

15. *Thou art a God that hidest thyself.*—A God that is unsearchable, whose ways, though excellent, are not as man's ways, and whose footsteps are not known.

19. *I have not spoken in secret.*—My oracles have not been hidden and ambiguous, my promises and threatenings have been distinct and clear. See note to c. 41, v. 24.

20. *Ye that are escaped of the nations.*—The great convulsion of Cyrus's conquests is supposed to be over, and the remnants of the conquered nations are called upon to leave their idols, and to know and acknowledge the God of Israel.

CHAPTER 46.

The idols of Babylon fall, and their captive worshippers, instead of being sustained by them, have to put them on beasts of burden to be carried; the God of Israel is no idol to be carried on beasts of burden or on men's shoulders, he carries his people. He has called Cyrus and will save Israel in his own manner.

1. *Bel boweth down, Nebo stoopeth.*—Babylonian idols. In the starworship of Babylon, Bel was the planet Jupiter; it has been conjectured that Nebo was the planet Mercury. The temple of Bel was one of the wonders of Babylon. The gods of the conquered people were carried off into captivity along with the people. So Jeremiah says (xlviii. 7) of Chemosh the god of Moab: "Chemosh shall go into captivity with his priests and his princes."

ib. *They are borne that ye carried.*—The Babylonians are addressed. The idols that they used to carry with honour in their religious processions, are now packed on horses and bullocks and borne by the weary beasts away.

2. *They could not deliver the burden.*—The false gods could not deliver their own images, borne into captivity.

8. *Shew yourselves men.*—Not such children as to confound me with these dumb idols, who cannot counsel or save.

11. *Calling an eagle from the east.*—Cyrus from Persia.

12. *Ye obdurate.*—Spoken to those Jews who were slow to believe in their deliverance through Cyrus.

CHAPTER 47.

An outburst of triumph on the approaching fall of luxurious, tyrannous, superstitious Babylon.

1. *Daughter of the Chaldeans.*—Chaldæa was the country, Babylon the capital.

2. *Take the millstones, &c.*—Perform the offices of a slave, thou who hast been so luxurious!

ib. *Uncover thy locks, &c.*—Struggle along on thy way into captivity, squalid and half-clad, thou who hast been so delicate!

6. *Upon the ancient.*—Israel. Israel *the ancient*, Israel *in his old age*, is used to heighten the picture of oppression. *Ancient* here must not be paralleled with *ancient* in c. 44, v. 7, "the ancient people;" the word in the original is not the same there as here, and means there *eternal*, God's chosen and eternal people.

9. *The loss of children and widowhood.*—Babylon is said to lose her children inasmuch as she loses her citizens, and to be a widow inasmuch as she loses her king.

ib. *The multitude of thy sorceries.*—The "magicians, astrologers, and sorcerers" of Babylon are familiar to us from the book of Daniel. See Dan. ii. 2.

14. *It shall not be a coal to warm at, &c.*—Not a pleasant, warmth-giving fire, but a devouring, destructive one.

15. *They with whom thou hast dealt.*—The magicians and astrologers of Babylon, with whose arts she has so busied herself, and on whom she has so relied, shall fail her in her day of trouble; they shall either be destroyed or flee.

CHAPTER 48.

Israel is warned against his old hardness of heart, and bidden to receive the declaration of that which is God's present will,—the deliverance of Israel through Cyrus. But for the wicked, let Israel know, there is no deliverance.

3. *I have declared the former things.*—Such as the fall of Assyria and of Babylon. See c. 41, v. 24, and the note there.

6. *Thou hast heard; see all this!*—The Vulgate well translates, *Quæ audisti, vide omnia!* All that was before prophesied to thee, the fall of these mighty kingdoms, behold it fulfilled!

ib. *I shew thee new things.*—What these "new things" are, namely, the deliverance through Cyrus, will be distinctly declared at v. 14.

11. *Will I do it.*—Deliver thee.
14. *Which among them.*—Among the false gods and the false prophets of the heathen.
ib. *The Lord hath loved him.*—*Him* is Cyrus. The Lord hath loved Cyrus; Cyrus will do the Lord's pleasure on Babylon, and the Lord's arm shall be, by Cyrus, on the Chaldeans.
16. *Come ye near unto me, &c.*—In this verse the Prophet, charged with these messages from God, speaks in his own name, and testifies to his countrymen that he has from the beginning pointed out to them God's hand and beck in these great events now happening.
21. *And they thirsted not, &c.*—This is what the delivered are to sing. On their return from Babylon, as in old time on their return from Egypt, they have been led safely through the desert and supplied with water.
22. *No peace.*—This is the note of warning, coming in at the close of the strain of promise.
At the end of this chapter there is a kind of pause in the discourse, which enters upon a second stage in the next chapter.

CHAPTER 49.

The Prophet, who had appeared in v. 16 of the preceding chapter, comes forth in this chapter more distinctly. Speaking in the name of Israel, the true Israel, the pious and persisting part of his nation, he announces God's calling and purposes for this Israel of whom he is the representative. God will not only restore the Jewish nation through this true Israel full of faith and of courage for the promised restoration; he will also bring the Gentiles to himself through its light and leading. It is true, many of the Jews are incredulous and desponding; vain are their fears; God will not forsake his people.

2. *He hath made my mouth like a sharp sword.*—Compare Heb. iv. 12: "The word of God is quick, and powerful, and sharper than any two-edged sword," &c.
6. *It is a light thing, &c.*—See the introduction to this chapter.
8. *A mediator of the people.*—The same expression as at c. 42, v. 6; see the note there. The people is the Jewish people as opposed to the Gentiles.
ib. *To establish the land.*—The Holy Land, which was to be restored and re-settled.
9. *The prisoners.*—The exiled and captive Israelites.
ib. *Their pastures shall be in all high places.*—See c. 41, v. 17, and the note there.
11. *My highways shall be exalted.*—Built up so as to form a clear and strong causeway to travel on.
12. *The land of Sinim.*—Probably China, which may have been known to the dwellers in Babylon as the name of a distant land, beyond India. It seems used here to imply the farthest parts of the world.
14. *But Zion said.*—The great body of the Jews were made despondent by their long adversity, and thought God had left them and would never restore them. Compare c. 40, v. 27: "Why sayest thou, O Jacob, and speakest, O Israel, My way is hid from the Lord, and my judgment is passed over from my God?"
16. *Graven thee upon the palms of my hands.*—As something to be ever remembered by me. See Deut. vi. 8: "And thou shalt bind them (God's words) for a sign upon thine hand, and they shall be as frontlets between thine eyes." Here the object for remembrance is conceived as written on something like paper, and then attached to the hands or face; in the text it is conceived as graven directly upon the hands. In Persia at this day people wear talismans, called *forms*, representing a star with five rays, each

ray having written on it an important text of the Koran, and in the middle of the star is written the name of God. These are now talismans, but they were originally *reminders*, to keep God and certain thoughts concerning him ever at hand. Their use throws light on the expressions, "to trust in God's *name*," "to fear the *name*," "to rejoice in the *name*," "to believe in the *name*," which so often occur in the Bible.

18. *All these.*—The scattered and exiled children of Zion.

19. *They that swallowed thee up.*—Zion's foreign conquerors and occupiers shall evacuate her, and leave her to her own children.

20. *The place is too strait for me.*—A picture of the fulness and prosperity, after her restoration, of the desolate and empty Jerusalem of the time of the exile.

21. *Then shalt thou say, &c.*—The expressions in this verse are to be closely noted, for the discourse returns to them at the beginning of the next chapter. Zion complains that she is, (1) a mother who has lost her children, and (2) a wife whom her husband (God) has abandoned.

24. *Shall the prey.*—Shall Israel be really rescued from such a power as Babylon? Yes.

CHAPTER 50.

In the first three verses the thread of the discourse is directly continued from the last chapter At v. 4 the Prophet, as the true Israel (see the introduction to the last chapter), speaks again of himself and his mission.

1. *Thus saith the Lord, &c.*—See v. 21 of the preceding chapter. Zion complains that her children are lost, and she is divorced. God answers: Can a writing of divorcement (St Matt. v. 31) be shown against me, as in a man's case, to prove a formal divorce? or, have I creditors to whom, as a human debtor, I sell my children? Zion is abandoned, and her children lost to her, but for a time, because of her sins and while her sins last.

2. *Wherefore, when I came, &c.*—The faint-heartedness of the bulk of the Jewish people, despondent and inert about the promised restoration, is rebuked, and God's almighty power to effect his designs is set forth.

10. *Who is among you.*—God speaks.

11. *Behold, all ye that kindle a fire.*—This is said to the Jews, who receive with incredulity, anger, and persecution, God's message and messenger. In this, as in the preceding verse, it is God who speaks: and he warns these Jews that their anger and violence shall be turned against themselves, and they shall "lie down in sorrow." See c. 66, v. 24.

CHAPTER 51.

This chapter continues the encouragement given at v. 10 of the preceding chapter. The faithful of Israel shall be brought to the land of promise like their father Abraham, and shall be blest and multiplied there; they shall be the means of extending God's salvation to the rest of the world. Let not man make them afraid; the Lord is with them, who brought them out of Egypt; who afflicted them, but will now save them and afflict their oppressors.

1. *The rock, &c.*—Abraham and Sarah, the progenitors of Israel.

2. *I called him alone.*—When he was but one, God called him, to make him a great nation. Compare Ezek. xxxiii. 24: "Abraham was one, and he inherited the land."

9. *Cut Rahab and wounded the dragon.*—Rahab, "the Proud," is Egypt; the dragon is probably the crocodile of the Nile, the emblematic beast of Egypt. As God smote Egypt of old, and delivered his people, so he will deliver them now.

12. *Afraid of a man.*—Such as thy oppressor, the king of Babylon, whom thou fearedst so, and who is now falling.

16. *That I may plant the heavens, &c.*—The new heavens and the new earth. Compare c. 65, v. 17.

18. *None to guide her.*—What follows is a picture of the misery wrought by Nebuchadnezzar's siege and destruction of Jerusalem.

19. *These two things.*—Desolation and destruction of the land is one of the two things; famine and slaughter of the people the other.

21. *Not with wine.*—Dizzy and staggering, not with wine, but with affliction from God.

23. *Laid thy body as the ground and as the street.*—A trait of the humiliation of the conquered and the insolence of the conqueror in Eastern kingdoms. So it is related that when Sapor king of Persia got on horseback, his prisoner, the Roman emperor Valerian, had to kneel down and make his back a step for him.

CHAPTER 52.

The strain of the previous chapter is continued. Israel shall be restored, and the mountains of Judah, and the waste places of Jerusalem, shall rejoice at the triumphal return to Zion of the Lord with his people. This strain ends with v. 12.

3. *Ye have sold yourselves for nought.*—This is the same sort of argumentation as at c. 50, v. 1; see the note there. Egypt and Assyria acquired no perpetual rights over Israel, they never became his purchasers and legal owners; so it is now with Babylon; Babylon has no permanent property in Israel whom it so heavily oppresses; therefore the Lord, who punished Israel by giving him over for a time to his enemies, will now restore him.

7. *Thy watchmen.*—The prophets, who with joy announce God's return with his redeemed people to Zion.

11. *From thence.*—From Babylon, on their march home to the Holy Land.

ib. The vessels of the Lord.—The holy vessels of the Temple, which had been carried off to Babylon, and which Cyrus restored to the returning Jews. See Ezra i. 7, 8: "Also Cyrus the king brought forth the vessels of the house of the Lord, which Nebuchadnezzar had brought forth out of Jerusalem, and had put them in the house of his gods; even those did Cyrus king of Persia bring forth by the hand of Mithredath the treasurer, and numbered them unto Sheshbazzar the prince of Judah."

12. *With haste.*—With haste and by flight, as ye did from Egypt. The exodus from Babylon shall be not like this, but public and triumphant.

13. *Behold my servant, &c.*—This and the two following verses belong to the next chapter. They declare the future glory of God's persecuted servant.

14. *His visage was so marred.*—See c. 50, v. 6.

15. *So shall many nations exult in him.*—The Vulgate has *asperget gentes multas*, "he shall sprinkle many nations:" and so, too, has our Bible. The Greek has: "Many nations shall be in admiration at him." The Chaldaic has, "he shall *rout*," or "*scatter*."

ib. Kings shall shut their mouths before him.—In sign of reverence.

CHAPTER 53.

The application of this well-known chapter to Christ will be in every one's mind. But it must be our concern here to find out its primary historical import, and its connection with the discourse where it stands. On this the 50th chapter throws much light; see particularly vv. 5—9. There we find ill usage and persecution of God's servant: "I gave my back to the smiters and my cheeks to them that plucked off the hair; I hid not my face from shame and spitting." In Jeremiah (c. 11, v. 19) we find this persecution of God's servant, at the hands of those who would not receive his word, threatening to proceed even to killing: "I was like a lamb or an ox that is brought to the slaughter; and I knew not that they had devised devices against me, saying, Let us destroy the tree with the fruit thereof, and let us cut him off from the land of the living, that his name may be no more remembered." From the same prophet we find that in the case of Urijah, brought from Egypt and put to death under Jehoiakim, the persecution *did* proceed even to killing (Jer. xxvi. 23). From the New Testament we learn the same thing: "Ye are witnesses unto yourselves, that ye are the children of them which killed the prophets;"—"Jerusalem, that killest the prophets" (St Matt. xxiii. 31, 37). Leaving the Bible, from Josephus we learn the same; from the Jewish traditions, too, the same. According to these traditions, Isaiah himself was put to death by Manasseh. Adding all this to the data furnished by this 53rd chapter itself, we have for the original subject of this chapter a martyred servant of God, recognisable by the Jews of the exile under the allusions here made to him, who eminently fulfilled the ideal of the servant of God, the true Israel, the mediator of the people and the light of the Gentiles, presented in this series of chapters; and whose death, crowning his life and reaching men's hearts, made an epoch of victory for this ideal.

More, as to the first and historical meaning, cannot be said with certainty. Many attempts have been made at an identification of this "man of sorrows" with his primary historical original, in addition to the identification of him with Christ; he has been said to be Hezekiah, Josiah, Isaiah himself, Jeremiah; but there are no sufficient grounds to establish his identity with any one of them.

The purport of the chapter is as follows. The Prophet, speaking as one of the Jewish people (as in c. 42, v. 24; "The Lord, he against whom *we* have sinned") declares how God's faithful servant, the bearer of his commands and promises, despised, persecuted, and at last taken away from prison and judgment to die, was stricken for the iniquities of the people, bare their sins, healed them by his sufferings, and would finally, in spite, nay, by means of his death, prevail and triumph.

1. *Who believed what we heard.*—See the last verse of the preceding chapter The Gentiles and their kings had never heard of God's servant; but we Jews, who heard and saw, had we more understanding?

ib. What we heard.—Literally, "our *hearing,*" which the Greek and the Vulgate have. The report *to us*, the report *we had* of God's commands and promises and of the glorification of his servant. See the last three verses of the preceding chapter; see also c. 49, vv. 1—8, and c. 50, vv. 7—11.

2. *Before him.*—Before the Lord.

ib. A slender plant.—The word in the original means merely a young shoot, a sapling. Not a *tender* plant, which implies beauty, delicacy and fostering care, but a *slender* plant, "as a root out of a dry ground," thin and insignificant.

3. *We hid as it were our faces.*—In contempt and disgust.

5. *The chastisement of our peace.*—The chastisement by which our peace is won.

7. *He was oppressed and he was afflicted.*—The Vulgate, which throughout this chapter translates so as to heighten the identification with Christ, has here: *Oblatus est quia ipse voluit*, He was offered because he himself chose to be. It is remarkable that in several places in this chapter the old Latin version which the Vulgate superseded is more faithful to the original than the Vulgate itself.

8. *He was taken, &c.*—Taken away from prison and from judgment to a violent death. This and the preceding verse are quoted in Acts viii. 32, 33, as the place of the Scripture which the Ethiopian eunuch was reading when Philip joined him. This verse is there quoted according to the Greek version, which mistakes the original: "In his humiliation his judgment was taken away, and who shall declare his generation? for his life is taken away from the earth."

ib. Who of his generation.—Who of his contemporaries recognised the true meaning of his death? that he died, not, as we thought, by his own fault, but for us and because of our sins.

ib. My people.—The Prophet speaks as in God's name. The Vulgate here makes God himself speak, and say: *Propter scelus populi mei percussi eum*, Because of the wickedness of my people I smote him.

9. *He made his grave with the wicked.*—Compare Jer. xxvi. 23, as to the burial of the prophet Urijah: "And they fetched forth Urijah out of Egypt and brought him unto Jehoiakim the king: who slew him with the sword, and cast his dead body into the graves of the common people."

11. *He shall see of the travail of his soul.*—He shall see the fruits of his sufferings in the many whom his life and death have turned to God and saved.

ib. By his knowledge.—Compare c. 50, v. 4: "The Lord God hath given me the tongue of the learned, that I should know how to speak a word in season to him that is weary," &c. In this and the following verse God himself speaks.

CHAPTER 54.

God's people thus purged and healed shall be eternally established, Israel shall extend his borders and multiply his sons; his enemies shall come over to him; this is the heritage of the servants of the Lord and their promised justification through God's righteous servant.

1. *Sing, O barren.*—Zion is addressed as at c. 49, vv. 18—21, and with the same promises. See the notes there. The captivity in Babylon is Zion's widowhood without her husband, the Lord; the slaughter and diminution of her people are her childlessness; this is to be more than made good after her restoration.

2. *Lengthen thy cords, &c.* Images taken from the pitching of tents.

6. *A wife of youth.*—And therefore beloved.

9. *This is as the waters of Noah unto me.*—I deal with my people respecting this their captivity in Babylon, as I dealt with them respecting Noah's flood. The words which follow explain the particular dealing meant.

15. *Whosoever shall gather together against thee, &c.*—It had been already promised that the Gentiles should resort to Israel for salvation; here it is added that even those who try to be his enemies shall come over to him.

16. *Behold I have created, &c.*—Destroyers and destruction are God's work; they reach those only whom he means them to reach, and he does not mean them to reach Israel.

17. *Their righteousness of me.*—This is what was promised at v. 11 of the preceding chapter: "By his knowledge shall my righteous servant justify many." In the original, the same word stands both for *justification* and for *righteousness*, and what is said here is: "This is the heritage of the servants of the Lord and their promised justification by me through means of my righteous servant."

CHAPTER 55.

The Jewish people are urged to take the freely offered salvation now close at hand; but are warned that they can have it only on condition of amending their lives.

1. *Ho, every one that thirsteth.*—Compare St John vii. 37: "Jesus stood and cried, saying, If any man thirst let him come unto me and drink."

3. *The sure mercies of David.*—The same sure, unfailing mercies which I showed to David.

4. *Behold, I appointed him.*—I gave formerly the nations into David's hand; so will I now into yours.

5. *Thou shalt call a nation, &c.*—See the preceding chapter, v. 3. See also c. 52, v. 15; and c. 45, v. 14, and the notes there.

12. *For ye shall go out with joy.*—On the return to the Holy Land. See c. 52, v. 12, and the note there.

CHAPTER 56.

The warning is continued. Righteousness is needed, in order to lay hold on God's coming salvation; but, with righteousness, the stranger may lay hold on it as well as Israel. At v. 8 the discourse turns abruptly, with severe threatenings, to the slothful and sinful part of the nation and their faithless guides.

1. *Do justice! for my salvation is near.*—This is nearly the same as John the Baptist's preaching, St Matt. iii. 2: "Repent ye, for the kingdom of heaven is at hand."

2. *That keepeth the sabbath.*—This seems at variance with Isaiah, c. 1, v. 13: "The new moons and sabbaths I cannot away with." But that related to a time when the kingdom of Judah yet stood, when the service of the Temple was in full course, the whole exterior part of the Jews' religion splendid and prominent; at such a time, a prophet might naturally under-value the whole of this exterior part in comparison with the inward part. But during the exile in Babylon all the services and sacrifices of the Temple had ceased, and the one testimony of faithfulness to their religion which the Jews among an idolatrous people could give was the observance of their Sabbath, their Sabbath was the one outward thing which brought their religion to their mind; hence its observance acquired quite a special value.

3. *Neither let the son of the stranger, &c.*—By the law of Moses, eunuchs and strangers were not to enter into the congregation of the Lord. See Deut. xxiii. 1—8. This exclusion was now to cease. A stricter and narrower policy, however, prevailed under Ezra and Nehemiah after the return (Neh. xiii. 14), and in general the views of the priesthood were, on a point like this, less liberal than those of the prophets. But our prophet's whole conception of the Gentiles in relation to the religion of Israel is unexampled in the Old Testament for its admirable width, depth and grandeur.

ib. Eunuch.—It must be remembered that, attached to a great Eastern court like that of Babylon, were a multitude of eunuchs, some of whom had perhaps adopted the religion of Israel. It is probable, also, that some of the Jewish youth were taken for the court service as eunuchs, and their country-men would afterwards have been likely to abhor them on that account. These considerations will enable us the better to feel the exquisite tender-ness and mercifulness of this passage.

5. *Better than of sons.*—A better and more enduring name than he could have had through children born to him to keep up his name and the name of his family.

7. *Mine house shall be called an house of prayer.*—The words quoted by Christ when he cleared the temple. See St Matt. xxi. 13.

9. *All ye beasts of the field.*—There is here an abrupt turn to the faithless part of the Jewish nation, under their negligent rulers and guides. The barbarous idolatrous nations are called, as beasts of the field and forest, to devour this easy prey.

10. *His watchmen.*—His chief men, princes, priests, and prophets.

CHAPTER 57.

The insensibility and idolatry of the unfaithful part of the Jewish nation are reproved. The restoration of Israel is, indeed, willed by God, but it is for the righteous only.

1. *The righteous perisheth, &c.*—We are taken back to the subject of c. 53: "Who of his generation regarded it, why he was cut off out of the land of the living?" The wicked cannot understand the meaning of the life and death of the righteous; how his perishing is not his fault, but the fault of the evil around him.

3. *But draw near, &c.*—The righteous dies and is at rest; but ye, what will ye make at last of your derision of the righteous, and of the follies and idolatries wherein ye trust? Nothing.

ib. Sons of the sorceress, &c.—Ye who have mixed yourselves up with the sorceries and idolatries of Babylon. The figure of adultery, &c., has reference to this idolatrous unfaithfulness. We find again in chapters 65 and 66 that many of the Jews in Babylon gave themselves to this, and thought it really religion and a way of safety out of their troubles.

4. *Against whom.*—The idolatrous Jews mocked and despised the pious and persisting servant of God.

5. *Under every green tree.*—The idolatrous worship in the consecrated groves of the false gods, so often mentioned in Scripture.

ib. Slaying the children in the valleys.—The most famous sacrifices of this kind were those in the valley of Hinnom. See Jeremiah vii. 31. They were made to Moloch, the king of heaven, the god of the Ammonites. But through all the kindreds of the Semitic race (to which the Babylonians, too, belonged) sacrifices of this sort seem to have been in use.

6. *They, they are thy lot.*—To them thou attachest thy luck, thy fortune. The worship of stones is a very early form of idolatry, and originated, probably, in the veneration paid to meteoric stones,—stones which, as the people said, "fell down from heaven." But the worship extended to other stones also. Traces of this worship occur twice in Genesis, in Jacob's consecration of the stones in his passage by Bethel, on his way to Mesopotamia and on his return thence. "And Jacob rose up early in the morning, and took the stone that he had put for his pillows, *and set it up for a pillar and poured oil upon the top of it.*" The Greeks, too, had this stone worship; "In the earlier times," says the Greek traveller Pausanias, "all the Greeks worshipped, in place of images of the gods, undressed stones." We find the name *Bætylia* given to these stones, and it has even been conjectured that this name comes from Bethel.

7. *Upon a lofty and high mountain.*—The worship "in high places" is well known.

ib. Thy bed.—The idolatry of the Jews is throughout spoken of under the figure of adultery, as unfaithfulness to God.

8. *Thy remembrance.*—Probably, small images like those of the Roman Penates or household gods, which were in every private family, and were the object of prayers and offerings.

ib. Thou hast enlarged thy bed.—Still the figure of adultery against God committed with the false gods of Babylon.

9. *And thou wentest, &c.*—See v. 5 and the second note there. The idolatrous Jews offered precious ointment and frankincense to Moloch. Moloch was the king of heaven, but these Jews sought out all idolatrous worships and false gods, down to the gods of the under-world.

10. *Thou art wearied.*—Nothing could convince these idolatrous Jews of the folly of their misplaced trust and vain worship.

11. *And of whom hast thou been afraid?*—How could thy calamities, and the fear of thy Babylonian tyrant, make thee so superstitious and forgetful?

14. *Cast ye up.*—As before; make a clear and smooth highway for my returning people.

15. *Of a contrite and humble spirit.*—This should be noted as, what may be called, *the new test* of religion, brought in,—or at any rate first set in clear light,—by this Prophet. See also c. 66, v. 2, where this *test* is again given. Compare, too, c. 42, v. 2.

19. *I create the fruit of the lips.*—I create comfort and joy of heart, and so give cause for the outpourings of praise and thankfulness from those whom I save.

ib. Peace to him that is far off.—Again this Prophet's large conception of the extent, reaching to the Gentiles as well as Jews, of God's salvation.

St Paul quotes these words in Eph. iii. 17: "Christ came and preached peace to you (the Gentiles) which were afar off, and to them that were nigh."

21. *No peace.*—Again this warning as to the sole condition upon which God's salvation can be had. See the last verse of c. 48.

CHAPTER 58.

Reproof continues. External worship is insufficient; a change of heart, mildness and mercy, are requisite in order that God's salvation offered to Israel may take effect.

1. *Cry aloud.*—God speaks to the prophet.

3. *Wherefore have we fasted?*—Besides the regular fasts of the Jewish religion, there were, during the captivity in Babylon, special fasts appointed as days of repentance and prayer for Israel.

ib. Exact all your labours.—Make your dependents do all the work you want done. Oppression, fault-finding, and harshness go on during the fast just the same.

4. *To be heard on high.*—If ye wish your voice and your prayer to be heard by God in heaven, this is not the sort of fast to induce him to listen.

9. *The putting forth of the finger.*—Mockery and insolence towards the pious and persisting part of the nation.

13. *The sabbath.*—For the special importance of the Sabbath during the captivity in Babylon see c. 58, v. 2, and the note there.

14. *The high places of the earth.*—In early times and in the warfare of early times the high and rocky situations were also the strong and defensible situations, and therefore he who occupied them was formidable and powerful.

CHAPTER 59.

Israel's sins are what make Israel's misery and defer his salvation; but God, because Israel is his chosen instrument, will himself interpose to break up the unrighteous kingdoms of the world and to restore Israel.

3. *Your hands are defiled.*—This and what follows is a picture of the sins of the unfaithful part of the Jewish nation during the captivity in Babylon, and in spite of the lessons taught by that captivity.

5. *They hatch cockatrice' eggs.*—They hatch mischief. Cockatrice is compounded of the words *cock* and *adder*, and is a fabled venomous serpent bred from an egg. Serpents do not lay eggs, but bring forth their young alive.

ib. Weave the spider's web.—They spin vain, foolish schemes, which can only come to nought.

7. *Their feet run to evil.*—Quoted in the Epistle to the Romans (iii. 15), to prove the guiltiness before God of the Jews under their law.

9. *Therefore is judgment gone from us.*—Here the person changes, and the Prophet speaks as himself one of the sinful people, and offers up in his own name and theirs a sort of confession of sins.

ib. We wait for light, &c.—See the preceding chapter, v. 3: "Wherefore have we fasted, and thou seest not?" Now the people know and confess the reason;—because of their sins.

10. *We grope for the wall.*—A picture of the helplessness and hopelessness of the Jewish exiles.

11. *We roar all like bears, and moan sore like doves.*—We complain loudly and obstreperously, and we complain with whining and moaning; in vain, because our heart is not right with God.

15. *He that departeth from evil maketh himself a prey.*—Again a reference, probably, to the subject of the 53rd chapter,—the death of the patient and innocent servant of God.

ib. And the Lord saw it, &c.—Israel, God's chosen instrument, failed to put down iniquity,—nay, himself fell into it: therefore God, by the wars and convulsions which shatter the world, will himself destroy the wicked, both Jew and Gentile, and will bring about, through these wars and convulsions, the restoration of Zion and of the remnant of the true Israelites, and the salvation of the world through the light that shall spring from them.

18. *According to their deeds, &c.*—The enemies of the Lord, whoever and wherever they are, Jew or Gentile, near or far, shall be visited and smitten.

19. *When the enemy.*—Cyrus. See c. 45, v. 1. Cyrus and his conquests are to be God's instruments of punishment to an unrighteous world, of restoration to the true Israelites.

20. *And a redeemer shall come to Zion, &c.*—The primary historical application of this is still to Cyrus, or, more strictly, to the salvation which was to arise for Zion, and through Zion for the world, out of that great storm of war and change in which Cyrus was the chief human agent. St Paul, in Rom. xi. 26, quotes the Greek version, which differs from the original: "'There shall come out of Sion the deliverer, and shall turn away ungodliness from Jacob." The best Greek text has not "out of Sion," as St Paul quotes, but "for Sion's sake."

21. *My spirit that is upon thee.*—The Prophet here declares God's promise to Israel that the line of prophets of God should not fail.

CHAPTER 60.

The Prophet, who has just announced "*A redeemer shall come to Zion,*" now describes Zion as it shall be after its restoration.

1. *Arise, shine.*—Zion is addressed; the Greek, the Vulgate, and the Chaldaic insert the explanatory word "Jerusalem."

2. *Darkness doth cover the earth.*—The kingdoms of the earth are breaking up amid gloom and misery; with Israel alone is light and joy in the Lord.

3. *And the Gentiles shall come to thy light.*—It shall be seen that Israel alone has in the Lord the secret of light and joy, and the heathen nations shall come to share it with Israel. See c. 45, v. 14, and the notes there.

4. *Thy sons shall come from far.*—See c. 49, v. 22: "The Gentiles... shall bring thy sons in their arms, and thy daughters shall be carried upon their shoulders." The nations amongst which the Jews are scattered shall bring them back to the Holy Land, with offerings and treasures to restore the Temple service and rebuild Jerusalem.

5. *The abundance of the sea.*—The riches of the coast-lands of the West, the Mediterranean countries, "the isles." More fully at v. 9.

6. *The multitude of camels.*—In this and the following verse are enumerated nations and contributions of the inland country to the south and south-east of Palestine, Arabian tribes and their respective products; in verses 8 and 9, those of the Mediterranean sea-board and the west. Midian and Ephah, with their caravan trade, Kedar (see c. 42, v. 11) and Nebaioth, with their flocks, are tribes of Northern Arabia; Sheba, with its gold and frankincense, is in Arabia Felix, to the south of them.

8. *Who are these that fly as a cloud?*—The Prophet has pictured the approach of the caravans of inland Arabia; now he pictures the approach of the fleets from the coast lands of the Mediterranean. The fleets with their sails, as seen afar off, are compared to a cloud, or to a flock of white doves flying towards their dovecote.

9. *Tarshish.*—The Greek Tartessus, a Phœnician settlement at the mouth of the Guadalquivir, outside the Straits of Gibraltar, and representing to the Hebrews the farthest west. It was the port whence the rich mineral produce of Spain was shipped by the Phœnicians.

11. *Therefore thy gates shall be open continually.*—This trait, with many others in the present chapter, is repeated in the picture of the new Jerusalem in the Book of Revelation (xxi. 25). Here the open gates have their special reason assigned: to admit the ever in-streaming world, with its offerings and homage.

12. *For the nation and kingdom.*—Every nation shall fall unless it serves the Lord, the righteous God, the God of Israel, through whom alone is salvation. The figure of serving Israel means serving the God of Israel.

13. *The glory of Lebanon.*—A reminiscence of the building of Solomon's temple, and of the contributions to it of cedar-wood out of Lebanon (1 Kings, v. 1—11), which are to be repeated now for the rebuilding of the Temple.

16. *Thou shalt also suck.*—See v. 11.

17. *For brass, &c.*—The more valuable, for the less valuable thou hast lost.

ib. *Thy officers peace.*—The restored Zion shall have peace-loving and righteous rulers.

21. *Thy people also shall be all righteous.*—The stress is on *all*. See c. 54, v. 13; c. 57, v. 13; and the twice-repeated warning: "No peace, saith my God, to the wicked!"

ib. *The branch.*—This is in apposition with *they*. They, the branch of my planting, the work of my hands, shall inherit the land for ever. In this and the concluding verse God himself speaks.

At the end of this chapter is a pause.

CHAPTER 61.

The Prophet speaks in his own name, as at c. 50, v. 4, which should be compared with the opening of this chapter. See also the opening of c. 49. He declares for whom his ministry and God's promises are intended, sums up the blessings of the new era at hand, and professes his joy and thankfulness for it.

1. *Unto the afflicted.*—The Vulgate, which the English Authorised Version follows, has *mansuetis*, "the meek;" the Greek has "the poor." It will be remembered how (St Luke iv. 18) Christ reads out this passage in the synagogue at Nazareth, and applies it to himself and his ministry. He quotes the Greek, and says "the poor."

ib. *Liberty to the captives.*—The expressions, "liberty to the captives," "opening of the prison to the bound," "acceptable year of the Lord," are all expressions with a special meaning for the Jews from the year of jubilee, when by the law of Moses the slave recovered his liberty. *Acceptable year* is more properly *gracious year*, or, *year of grace of the Lord.*

3. *Beauty for ashes.*—Beauty means *ornament* here; the signs of joy instead of the signs of mourning.

5. *And strangers.*—The Jews, a nation of God's servants appointed to initiate the rest of the world into his service, are to give themselves to this sacred and priestly labour, while the rest of the world do their secular labour for them.

7. *For your shame ye shall have double.*—See c. 40, v. 1: "Jerusalem receiveth of the Lord's hand double for all her rue."

ib. *My people.*—One of the sudden changes of person so common with this Prophet. *Ye* and *they* both relate to God's people, Israel.

10. *I will greatly rejoice.*—The Prophet speaks as already possessing by anticipation the blessings promised, and as filled with gratitude for them.

CHAPTER 62.

For these blessings the Prophet will not cease to pray and wrestle, until they arrive, and the glorious salvation of the renewed Zion shines forth.

1. *Righteousness.*—More properly here *saving health*. The Vulgate, to make the application to Christ evident, translates: "Until her *Just One* go forth as brightness, and her *Saviour* be lighted as a lamp."

2. *New name.*—We have again, in the Book of Revelation, this bestowal of a *new name* upon those whom God has redeemed and renewed.

4. *My delight is in her, and thy land Married.*—In the Hebrew, Hephzibah and Beulah.

6. *I have set watchmen.*—God declares that he has set his watchmen, his angels, upon the walls of Jerusalem, to remind him of her continually. Compare c. 49, v. 16. The Prophet entreats these watchmen to ply their office without ceasing, until Jerusalem is restored.

10. *Go through, go through.*—Compare c. 40, v. 3. The immediate return of the Lord with his chosen people to Jerusalem, is announced, and preparations for the triumphal march and entry are to be made.

ib. Lift up a standard for the nations.—In order that "the Gentiles shall come to thy light, and kings to the brightness of thy rising." See c. 60, v. 3.

CHAPTER 63.

So sure are God's purposes that even if mortal instruments (such as Cyrus) fail, God himself will do the work upon the enemies of Israel. The Prophet selects Edom as a kindred and neighbour people of Israel, and yet their ancient and specially bitter enemy (compare c. 34; compare also Ezek. xxxv. 5, and Ps. cxxxvii. 7), who had assisted Nebuchadnezzar in the destruction of Jerusalem. In a kind of short drama, of sublime grandeur, the Prophet exhibits God himself as returning from executing vengeance upon Edom.

After the 6th verse the subject changes, and the Prophet, reverting to God's old mercies towards Israel, supplicates for their renewal.

1. *Who is this?*—A conqueror with blood-stained garments is supposed to appear. The spectators ask, Who is he?—He is the Lord.

ib. Bozrah.—A place in Hauran, to the north of Edom as marked in the maps, but the territory of the Edomites reached there after the downfall of the Jewish kingdom. Bozrah, or Bostra, afterwards became a place of importance; the fairs of Bozrah and Damascus are mentioned as the two great Syrian fairs which Mahomet in his youth visited.

ib. I that speak.—God answers. In the next verse the spectators again question; in the three following verses God speaks.

4. *I looked, and there was none to help.*—The year of God's redeemed has come (see c. 61, v. 1, and the note there), the time for the restoration of Israel that the world might be saved through Israel; the kings of the earth and the revolutions of states might fail or delay in bringing about God's designs for Israel; then God himself must interpose.

7. *I will mention.*—Here the short drama, or vision, of the Divine Conqueror of Edom ends; the Prophet reverts to God's old loving-kindnesses and the deliverance from Egypt, and implores a return of like dealings of God with Israel.

13. *As an horse in the desert.*—As the free, light-stepping horse of the Arab in the desert.

14. *As the beast.*—As the cattle go instinctively down to sheltered places for their rest, so Israel was led to places of rest and security.

15. *The sounding of thy bowels.*—The metaphor is from strings lightly stretched, and giving, therefore, a louder and deeper sound.

16. *Though Abraham be ignorant of us.*—Though we are in exile, strangers to the Holy Land and the polity founded by our fathers.

18. *Our adversaries.*—Babylon and the heathen nations.

CHAPTER 64.

The supplication goes on without interruption, but it passes into a confession of sins in the name of the whole people,—sins that had grown up amidst the despair and misery of the exile,—and ends with an appeal to God's grace and mercy.

1. *That thou wouldest rend the heavens.*—That thou wouldest appear once more in fire, as formerly on Sinai.

4. *Who hath prepared.*—Before *who* supply, to complete the sense, *a God*.
5. *That rejoiceth.*—In the Lord. Compare Psalm xcvii. 12: "*Rejoice in the Lord*, ye righteous."
ib. *Wroth with them continually.*—With thy people Israel. One of the changes of person already noticed as frequent with this Prophet.

CHAPTER 65.

God makes answer to the foregoing supplication. He has called his people, but in vain; they have been obstinately deaf to him, unfaithful and superstitious. The unfaithful shall be punished; but a faithful remnant shall be saved and restored to Zion, and for them the promises shall take effect.

1. *I gave ear to them, &c.*—Quoted from the Greek version, but with a transposition of the two clauses, by St Paul in the Epistle to the Romans, x. 20: "I was found of them that sought me not, I was made manifest unto them that asked not after me." St Paul applies this verse to the Gentiles, and the verse following to Israel. Here both verses apply to Israel.
3. *Gardens.*—The gardens and sacred groves of the false gods. See c. 1, v. 29: "Ye shall be confounded for the gardens that ye have chosen."
ib. *The tiles.*—The roof-tiles of the flat-roofed Eastern houses, where the Chaldeans practised their star-worship. See Zephaniah, i. 4, 5: "I will cut off them that worship the host of heaven upon the housetops."
4. *Remain among the graves, &c.*—The Greek adds, in explanation, "for the sake of visions." What is meant is the heathen practice called *incubatio*,—passing the night on tombs or in sacred places for the sake of apparitions and revelations expected there.
ib. *Which eat swine's flesh, &c.*—Which use for their sacrifices, and for their feasts after their sacrifices, things unclean and forbidden to Israel.
5. *Which say, Stand by thyself.*—Yet doing all this out of superstition, and out of the vain notion that it will be of religious avail to them, they insolently repel their unsuperstitious and faithful brethren as less holy than themselves.
6. *These are a smoke in my nose, &c.*—Make my nostrils to smoke with wrath, and my wrath to burn like fire.
7. *Burned incense upon the mountains, &c.*—The so often mentioned idolatrous worship upon the high places. See c. 57, v. 7.
8. *As the new wine, &c.*—The juice that shall one day be wine is in the grape-cluster, and the grape-cluster is preserved for its sake; so Israel shall be preserved, for the sake of the life and blessing to come from it.
9. *My mountains.*—The mountains of Judah in general, and the hills of Zion and Moriah in particular.
10. *Sharon.*—The strip of western coast from Joppa northwards to Cæsarea. The valley of Achor is opposed to it, as being in the east of the Holy Land, by Jericho.
11. *Fortune.*—In the original, *Fortune* and *that which destineth* are Gad and Meni. Gad means *luck*, Meni means *fate* or *destiny*. They are Babylonian names of two stars, or, star-deities; probably of the two planets held to be fortunate, Jupiter and Venus. Or, Meni may be the planet Saturn, the unlucky star, opposed to Jupiter, the star of good luck.
15. *By another name.*—A name like, *The blessed of the Lord*. See v. 23.
17. *I create new heavens.*—With the break-up of the heathen kingdoms and the restoration of Israel begins a new epoch.
20. *There shall be no more, &c.*—Child and man shall alike attain to a patriarchal age. The child shall grow up and come to old age; the sinner shall be an old man when his curse overtakes him.
22. *As the days of a tree.*—Man's life shall have, instead of its present brief term, the far longer term allotted to the life of trees.

25. *Dust shall be the serpent's meat.*—The serpent shall be harmful no more, but shall be content to feed on dust, an innocent food.

CHAPTER 66.

The discourse is continued from the preceding chapter.

God declares his chief pleasure to be in piety; the sacrifices of the superstitious and unfaithful Jews shall avail them nothing, while, on the other hand, the triumph of their faithful brethren is immediately approaching. Swiftly shall Zion rise again from her ruins; then shall be held a day of the Lord to sift the unfaithful from among the righteous, and to punish them and all their like; the whole world shall afterwards flow to Zion and worship before God.

1. *The heaven is my throne, &c.*—Stephen quotes this in his speech before the council. After saying, "Howbeit the most High dwelleth not in temples made with hands," he goes on, "As saith the prophet," and quotes this passage. See Acts vii. 48—50.

2. *But to this man, &c.*—See c. 57, v. 15. The line of thought seems to be as follows: The temple is going to be rebuilt, and men's thoughts will be concentrated upon this work made with hands; in Babylon the unfaithful Jews have just shown, by even adopting the rites and sacrifices of the heathen, how prone men are to rely upon the outward parts of religion; at this moment, therefore, God will declare that what he regards is not these things, but inward religion; lowliness, contrition, and awe of his word.

3. *He that killeth an ox.*—These superstitious Jews in Babylon, who thought to be more religious than their brethren by multiplying ceremonies and sacrifices, even those of the heathen, included in the jumble of observances to which they were thus led rites the most abominable, far more than enough to countervail the other sacrifices by which they thought, perhaps, to replace the suspended worship of the Temple; to this their superstitious unfaithfulness and self-will brought them, and to a neglect or violation of all that God really regards.

5. *Ye that tremble at his word.*—This is addressed to the faithful part of the nation. Their superstitious brethren had scornfully repelled them, thinking that they glorified God by doing so, and by multiplying the observances which constituted, they hoped, their own superior holiness: God was indeed about to be glorified, but by the restoration of Zion and the triumph of the faithful few, to the discomfiture of the faint-hearted clingers to Babylon.

6. *A voice of noise, &c.*—The restoration is supposed to be taking place. The three following verses describe its incomparable suddenness and rapidity.

12. *The glory of the Gentiles.*—See c. 60, v. 5.

14. *The hand of the Lord, &c.*—When Zion is rebuilt the Lord will hold a great day of judgment there, to sift out and punish his enemies.

15. *The gardens.*—As before, the consecrated groves and gardens of the heathen deities.

ib. *One chief in the midst.*—The *choragus* or ringleader in the idolatrous processions and ceremonies.

16. *All flesh.*—Not the Jews only, but *all flesh;* and the wicked of *all flesh* shall perish.

17. *Swine's flesh.*—Such uncleanness and abomination for Israel as has already been mentioned at v. 3, and in c. 65, v. 4, and in c. 57, vv. 5—9.

18. *It shall come.*—After this vengeance on the wicked God will gather the world to Zion to see his glory and to worship him.

19. *Those that escape of them.*—See c. 45, v. 20: "Assemble yourselves ... ye that are escaped of the nations." See also v. 14 of the same chapter. Those who remain of the nations, after the wars and destructions coming upon the earth, having been converted themselves to the God of Israel, shall go to all parts of the world spreading God's name, and setting at

liberty the widely dispersed Israelites, whom they shall bring back to Jerusalem as an offering to the Lord.

ib. Tarshish, Phul, and Lud, &c.—The prophet goes from west to east in his enumeration. For Tarshish see c. 60, v. 9, and the note there. Phul is the country mentioned with Lud in Ezekiel, xxvii. 10, and by him there called Phut, where the Greek and the Vulgate translate *Libyans*. In the text now before us the Greek has Phud or Phut after the Hebrew, but the Vulgate translates *Africa*. An African people is meant, and an African people famous in the use of the bow, which the Ethiopians, for example, were. Lud is Lydia, the well-known western kingdom of Asia Minor, conquered by Cyrus before his march against Babylon. Tubal is a people in the north-east of Asia Minor. Javan is Greece, Ionia; Homer has the word Iaones, which is very near Javan; and a Greek note-writer to another poet says: "The barbarians call all the Greeks *Iaones*." The *sign* mentioned at the beginning of this verse consists in the converted Gentiles going to convert the more distant heathen world, and to bring the scattered Israelites home.

20. *And they shall bring, &c.*—Compare c. 43, v. 5; and c. 49, v. 12 and v. 22.

ib. An offering.—The restored Israelites shall be offered by their Gentile liberators to the Lord in Zion, as gifts are offered to the Temple.

21. *For priests and for Levites.*—Of the Gentiles also shall priests and Levites for God's service be taken. Originally priests and Levites had been taken from the tribe of Levi only, but at c. 61, v. 6 it was said of the Israelites generally: "Ye shall be named the priests of the Lord; men shall call you the ministers of our God." And now, finally, our Prophet's horizons widen yet more, and he admits to the priesthood and ministry of God the Gentiles also.

23. *From one new moon, &c.*—Every new moon and every sabbath shall all flesh, Gentile as well as Jew, worship before the Lord.

24. *The men that have transgressed.*—The unfaithful and unrighteous who in the day of God's judgment have been separated and slain. See v. 16.

ib. Their worm shall not die, &c.—This expression is adopted in the New Testament: "Where their worm dieth not and their fire is not quenched" (St Mark ix. 44).

Cambridge:

PRINTED BY C. J. CLAY, M.A.
AT THE UNIVERSITY PRESS.

By Rev. G. F. MACLEAR, B.D.,
Head Master of King's College School, London.

A Class-Book of Old Testament History. Sixth Edition. With Four Maps. 18mo., 4s. 6d.

A Class-Book of New Testament History. With Four Maps. Fourth Edition. 18mo., 5s. 6d.

A Class-Book of the Catechism of the Church of England. Second Edition. 18mo., 2s. 6d.

A First Class-Book of the Catechism. With Scripture Proofs. For Junior Classes and Schools. 18mo., 6d.

A Shilling Book of Old Testament History. For National and Elementary Schools. 18mo.

A Shilling Book of New Testament History. 18mo.

The Order of Confirmation. For the Use of Candidates. With suitable Devotions and Collects. 18mo., 3d.

MACMILLAN AND CO. LONDON.

Bible Lessons. By the Rev. E. A. ABBOTT, M.A. Head Master of the City of London School. Second Edition. Crown 8vo., 4s. 6d.

Scripture Readings for Families and Schools. By CHARLOTTE M. YONGE, Author of "The Heir of Redclyffe."

FIRST SERIES. Genesis to Deuteronomy. Extra fcap. 8vo., 1s. 6d. Also with Comments, 3s. 6d.

SECOND SERIES. Joshua to Solomon. Extra fcap. 8vo., 1s. 6d. Also with Comments, 3s. 6d.

The Golden Treasury Psalter. Student's Edition. Being an Edition with briefer Notes of the "Psalms chronologically arranged by Four Friends." 18mo., 3s. 6d.

The Sunday Book of Poetry for the Young. Selected and arranged by C. F. ALEXANDER. 18mo., 4s. 6d.

An Elementary Introduction to the Book of Common Prayer. By the Rev. F. PROCTER, M.A. and the Rev. G. F. MACLEAR, B.D. With an Explanation of the Morning and Evening Prayer and the Litany. Fourth Edition. 18mo., 2s. 6d.

MACMILLAN AND CO. LONDON.

www.ingramcontent.com/pod-product-compliance
Lightning Source LLC
Chambersburg PA
CBHW020148170426
43199CB00010B/943